Eliot in His Time

This volume is published in cooperation with The English Institute. The essays by Robert M. Adams, Hugh Kenner, Michael Goldman, and Donald Davie were read at the thirty-first session of the Institute, Harvard University, September 2-5, 1972.

Eliot in His Time

ESSAYS ON THE OCCASION OF THE FIFTIETH ANNIVERSARY OF *THE WASTE LAND*

A. WALTON LITZ, *Editor*

HUGH KENNER

RICHARD ELLMANN

HELEN GARDNER

ROBERT LANGBAUM

ROBERT M. ADAMS

MICHAEL GOLDMAN

DONALD DAVIE

PRINCETON UNIVERSITY PRESS
PRINCETON, NEW JERSEY

Copyright © 1973
by Princeton University Press
L.C. Card: 72-4046
I.S.B.N.: 0-691-06240-4
All rights reserved.
The essay by Richard Ellmann, "The
First *Waste Land*," is reprinted with
permission from *The New York Review
of Books*. Copyright © 1971 Richard
Ellmann. Portions of the essay by
A. Walton Litz, "*The Waste Land* Fifty
Years After," first appeared in the
Journal of Modern Literature, and are
reprinted by permission.
Selections from the poetry, plays, and
essays of T. S. Eliot and from *The Waste
Land: A Facsimile and Transcript*
edited by Valerie Eliot are reprinted by
permission of Harcourt Brace Jovan-
ovich, Inc.; copyright, 1932, 1935,
1936, 1950, by Harcourt Brace Jovano-
vich, Inc.; copyright, © 1950, 1962,
1963, by T. S. Eliot; copyright, © 1971
by Valerie Eliot.
Publication of this book has been
aided by the Whitney Darrow
Publication Reserve Fund of
Princeton University Press.
Printed in the United States of America
by Princeton University Press,
Princeton, New Jersey.
second printing, 1974

Contents

Eliot in His Time

A. Walton Litz *THE WASTE LAND*
FIFTY YEARS AFTER

THE FIFTIETH anniversary of
the publication of T. S. Eliot's
The Waste Land is an obvious occasion for critical revalu-
ation. Already we are separated from the great works of
that *annus mirabilis*, 1922, by a distance in time and
sensibility as great as that which separated Eliot and
Pound and Joyce from their Victorian predecessors. In
the late 1940's, when I first encountered *The Waste
Land*, I could still read Eliot as if he were my contem-
porary: evidence both of the extraordinary impact of the
"modernist" movement and of *The Waste Land*'s central
place in that movement. Few works can have remained
avant-garde for so long. But now that "modernism" has
passed into the realm of literary history *The Waste Land*
must pass with it, helped on its way by the recent dis-
covery and publication of the original manuscripts and
typescripts. *The Waste Land* and Eliot's other poems will
never look quite the same again.

To me *The Waste Land* has always been the classic
example of the "really new" work of art, as Eliot himself
describes it in "Tradition and the Individual Talent": the

3

radical achievement which enters the established order of literary works and causes a permanent shift in our perspective, so that the entire idea of a literary tradition is significantly altered. This position of The Waste Land as the central or normative statement of a new literary age was recognized from the start. In July 1922, three months before the poem's publication, Ezra Pound wrote to his former teacher Felix E. Schelling that "Eliot's Waste Land is I think the justification of the 'movement,' of our modern experiment, since 1900." Like Joyce's Ulysses, The Waste Land was acknowledged as a revolutionary document while still a work in progress. It was part of the propaganda, as well as the crowning achievement, of the "new poetry" of 1909-1922.

A moment ago I referred to my own first reading of Eliot as an encounter with a "contemporary": I suspect that the contributors to this volume belong to the last generation which could confront him on that particular ground. The experience of The Waste Land as a contemporary poem now belongs to literary history, although—interestingly enough—the same cannot be said for that other master-document of 1922, Joyce's Ulysses. As Richard Ellmann remarks in the opening sentence of his great biography, "We are still learning to be James Joyce's contemporaries," and all the criticism of this anniversary year seems to bear him out. The burden of this year's conferences, reviews, and articles has been that we are still learning to read Ulysses, whereas in the case of Eliot the time has come for "revaluation" and placing. Whether we believe that Eliot was the Arnold of his age, or perhaps the Cowley, the time for such judgments has come. If the essays in this collection are linked together by a major theme, that theme is the need for reassessment and revaluation.

4

As several of the following essays testify, the facsimile publication of Eliot's drafts and revisions for *The Waste Land* has done more than reveal the latent possibilities in the finished poem: it has made us all aware of the critical slogans and textbook schemas which produced, over the past twenty-five years, a "standard" interpretation of *The Waste Land* that has colored our view of Eliot's entire achievement. Most critics of the poem— lured by its surface complexity and the intriguing notes —have treated *The Waste Land* as a sacred text in need of an ordinary gloss, thus delivering a critical model more orderly, more "traditional," and more moralistic than the poem itself. And this standard or normative reading of *The Waste Land* has, in turn, distorted our understanding of the later poetry and drama.

The first cause of this distorting process appears to have been Eliot's well-known review of Joyce's *Ulysses* ("*Ulysses*, Order, and Myth," published in *The Dial* in November 1923), which was taken to mean that Eliot and Joyce had employed the same "mythical method." Here is the crucial passage in Eliot's essay:

"In using the myth, in manipulating a continuous parallel between contemporaneity and antiquity, Mr. Joyce is pursuing a method which others must pursue after him. They will not be imitators, any more than the scientist who uses the discoveries of an Einstein in pursuing his own, independent, further investigations. It is simply a way of controlling, of ordering, of giving a shape and a significance to the immense panorama of futility and anarchy which is contemporary history. . . . It is a method for which the horoscope is auspicious. Psychology (such as it is, and whether our reaction to it be comic or serious), ethnology, and *The Golden Bough* have concurred to make possible what was impossible even a few

5

years ago. Instead of narrative method, we may now use the mythical method. It is, I seriously believe, a step toward making the modern world possible for art . . ."

The implications of this passage would seem to be quite clear. As Thomas Mann once said, the task of the modern artist is to convert the individual and the bourgeois into the typical and the mythical, and *Ulysses* showed Eliot one way to accomplish such a transformation. As assistant editor of the *Egoist* and close reader of the *Little Review*, the magazines in which the early chapters of *Ulysses* appeared serially, Eliot would have been familiar with Joyce's use of myth by late 1919; and the delicate exchanges between past and present in *The Waste Land* obviously owe a great deal to Joyce's method. Nonetheless, there are sharp differences between the use of the *Odyssey* in *Ulysses* and the use of the Grail legend in *The Waste Land*, differences that are often overlooked. They are brought into focus by Eliot's comment that the mythical method can be used as a substitute for the effects of conventional narration. In Joyce's novel the *Odyssey* provides an hypothetical or ideal plot as well as a fixed standard of human psychology, a plot that parallels or counterpoints the contemporary action; but the Grail legend, as retold by Jessie Weston, supplies not a plot but a structure of values (or, if you will, a ritualistic norm). In treating Eliot's use of the Grail legend as if it were analogous to Joyce's use of the *Odyssey*, many critics have supplied *The Waste Land* with a spurious plot which exists outside the poem, and which fosters the mistaken notion that *The Waste Land* (like a five-act tragedy) moves from conflict through reversal into some sort of resolution. What is essentially an internal drama is turned by this method into an external quest whose outcome can only be fragmentary or inconclusive. In sum, the leading critics of the poem have too often produced a temporal rather than a spatial pattern, and have discerned a set of moralistic judgments on life where nothing was intended but a delicate balance of attitudes. Just as the early defenders of *Ulysses* overemphasized the novel's mechanical orders as a defense against philistine charges of "formlessness" or "chaotic construction," so the early admirers of *The Waste Land* were determined to give every line a moral meaning in order to rescue Eliot from charges of negativism and nihilism. The result has too often been a programmatic interpretation that makes *The Waste Land* seem little different from the ironic Sweeney poems or "Burbank with a Baedeker." Much might be gained if readers of *The Waste Land* could, for a few years, adopt the motto Mark Twain affixed to *Huckleberry Finn*: "persons attempting to find a moral in [this work] will be banished; persons attempting to find a plot in it will be shot."

It would be my contention that the essential life of *The Waste Land* does not lie in the obvious contrasts between past and present which inform most of the set pieces. The famous description of the modern woman at her dressing table ("The Chair she sat in, like a burnished throne,/ Glowed on the marble . . .") is less interesting for what it tells us about Cleopatra and her modern counterpart than for what we learn about Eliot's conception of heroic verse. Nor does the quick of the poem lie in the broad thematic contrasts between two kinds of life and two kinds of death, the dual symbolisms of fire and water. If this were so, *The Waste Land* would be fit only for courses on religious ideas in literature. *The Waste Land* is not *about* spiritual dryness, it is about the ways in which that dryness can be perceived and expressed. Like Ezra Pound's *Hugh Selwyn Mauberley*, it is a museum of verse forms,

7

an experiment with language, the record of a special
sensibility exposed to the anxieties of a particular culture.
Perhaps it would be best if we refrained, at least for a
little while, from thinking of *The Waste Land* as a major
revelation of modern man's spiritual plight—"an *Inferno*
which looked towards a *Purgatorio*"—and thought of it
as a master document of the modernist movement in lit-
erature, a work that both culminates the movement and
performs an act of criticism upon it.

Once freed from its burden of spiritual significance,
the poem can then be approached in a variety of ways,
and with more humor and tact than it has usually re-
ceived. The satiric turns in the manner of Pound's verses
on contemporary manners; the parodies and ventriloquial
effects of the English music hall; the oblique comments
on the foreground of English poetry; the persistent strain
of Augustan irony; the combination of a precise topog-
raphy with a dream landscape; the vindication of poetry
as ritual and mystery; the violent yoking of realism and
surrealism; literary variations on the effects of collage
Cubism; montage techniques borrowed from the reper-
toire of the early cinema—these aspects and many more
would have to be explored in any analysis of *The Waste
Land* that aimed at balance and completeness. The ques-
tion is really one of where to begin, and what to empha-
size. So as one step toward establishing critical priorities,
I would like to take up the vexed question of the notes
to the poem and Eliot's use of "sources," topics that lead
directly to a consideration of how *The Waste Land*
achieved its present unity of form in the months of late
1921 and early 1922.

When *The Waste Land* was first published in magazine
form in the autumn of 1922 it was free of annotation:

the notes to the poem were added—according to Ezra Pound—at the express wish of the first book publisher, Liveright, who "wanted a longer volume and the notes were the only available unpublished matter." Evidently Eliot's attitude toward the entire apparatus of references and sources, like that of most of his readers, was ambiguous from the start. The fundamental notes were never, of course, a hoax or a publisher's gimmick; they existed in private form during the writing of the poem, and were used by Eliot's friends as *The Waste Land* circulated in typescript. In this sense, the original notes were an integral part of the poem, not unlike the elaborate chart of symbolic correspondences and Homeric parallels that Joyce circulated privately for the benefit of the first readers of *Ulysses*. It is interesting and revealing that these two great monuments of the modernist movement, published in the same year, should have come into the world trailing their own guides to interpretation. Obviously, Joyce's *schema* and Eliot's notes were part of the "cultic" atmosphere that surrounded both writers. They were the top-secret information needed for any successful revolution; they flaunt the fact that modern literature must be intricate and difficult, that it involves hard intellectual effort, and that for a time it must be nurtured by a coterie of those who know. So at bottom, Eliot's later regrets that the notes were so widely circulated have nothing to do with the validity of the notes themselves, but rather with their effect on the general audience once they escaped the hands of the initiated. Like Joyce's *schema*, once it was revealed by Stuart Gilbert, the notes had a centrifugal effect on most criticism, driving the reader away from the work and into ever-widening circles of source-study and influence-charting.

In his 1956 lecture on "The Frontiers of Criticism"

(later published in *On Poetry and Poets*) Eliot made his best-known comment on the notes, a comment remarkable both for its distortion of the original circumstances and for its implication that only the critics have been led into temptation, while the initiated—Eliot's fellow poets—have known how to handle the information.

"Here I must admit that I am, on one conspicuous occasion, not guiltless of having led critics into temptation. The notes to *The Waste Land*! I had at first intended only to put down all the references for my quotations, with a view to spiking the guns of critics of my earlier poems who had accused me of plagiarism. Then, when it came to print *The Waste Land* as a little book—for the poem on its first appearance in *The Dial* and in *The Criterion* had no notes whatever—it was discovered that the poem was inconveniently short, so I set to work to expand the notes, in order to provide a few more pages of printed matter, with the result that they became the remarkable exposition of bogus scholarship that is still on view today. I have sometimes thought of getting rid of these notes; but now they can never be unstuck. They have had almost greater popularity than the poem itself—anyone who bought my book of poems, and found that the notes to *The Waste Land* were not in it, would demand his money back. But I don't think that these notes did any harm to other poets. . . ."

The "bogus scholarship" Eliot refers to is easily identified by any scholar from his own experience: the lengthy quotation from Ovid, in the original Latin; the passage from Chapman's *Handbook of Birds of Eastern North America*; the reference to a pamphlet on *The Proposed Demolition of Nineteen City Churches*—these and similar references are the devices we all use from time to time to dress up or pad out our own work, and they have led

10

to the notion that Eliot's notes are a parody of scholarship (the apparatus of *The Waste Land* so infuriated William Carlos Williams that he could think of *Paterson* as "a reply to Greek and Latin with the bare hands"). Many of the notes *are* "bogus," but only in their lack of proportion. As I shall illustrate in a few moments, every detail in the notes—no matter how trivial—refers to some stage in the imaginative growth of the poem. The problem is not whether to accept or reject the information, but how to weigh and use it. This is exactly the problem Eliot is getting at, obliquely, in "The Frontiers of Criticism," which might have been subtitled: "An attempt to establish sensible frontiers for criticism of *The Waste Land*."

"The Frontiers of Criticism" is a deeply divided essay, divided by the tension between Eliot's critical theory on the one hand (which rejects any attempt to trace the work of art back into its origins, and sees the work as self-sufficient and autonomous), and on the other his own poetic practice and that of his contemporaries (which relies explicitly on the identification of allusions and the recognition of echoes). In the essay Eliot focuses his concern on two works that seem to him to lie beyond the frontiers of normal criticism: one is John Livingston Lowes's famous source study, *The Road to Xanadu*; the other is Joyce's *Finnegans Wake*. *The Road to Xanadu* fascinated Eliot because, for all its seductive interest (really the interest one has in a piece of detection), it dramatizes a radical and irreducible gap between the writer's sources and his finished creation. Lowes, like Coleridge, was an omnivorous reader, and in *The Road to Xanadu* he traces to their originals the countless "borrowed images or phrases" that make up the texture of *Kubla Khan* and *The Ancient Mariner*. But in spite of the

11

vast amount of fascinating material thrown up by Lowes's research, the book has almost no "critical" value. As Eliot comments, "No one, after reading this book, could suppose that he understood *The Ancient Mariner* any better." Nor does the book add much to our knowledge of the creative imagination: when faced with the actual process by which Coleridge's reading was transformed into art, all Lowes can do is quote Ariel's song from *The Tempest*, mutter something about a sea-change, and pass by. Eliot himself can do no better, since—when discussing Coleridge in *The Use of Poetry and the Use of Criticism*—he remarks that the imagery of *Kubla Khan*, "whatever its origins in Coleridge's reading, sank to the depths of Coleridge's feeling, was saturated, transformed there—'those are pearls that were his eyes'—and brought up into daylight again."

So *The Road to Xanadu*, as Eliot reads it, would seem to place a bar before most source-hunting and genetic criticism, warning us away from the manuscript evidence and the direction pointed out by the notes to *The Waste Land*. And yet there is the troubling presence of *Finnegans Wake*, that pyrrhic victory of the major tendencies in modernist art, where the process of composition is part of the book's subject-matter, and where the sources are an indispensable—one might almost say the sole—route to the work's structure and meaning. It is no accident that the best critical studies of *Finnegans Wake*, Clive Hart's *Structure and Motif in "Finnegans Wake"* and J. S. Atherton's *The Books at the Wake*, are source-studies reminiscent of Lowes.

So here is the puzzle of a critical theory that resists any attempt to explain poetry "in terms of something else," coupled with a poetic technique that constantly drives our attention toward other works or toward the poet's private experience. Eliot confesses in the same essay that his own best criticism consists of "essays on poets and poetic dramatists who had influenced me," and is "a by-product of my private poetry-workshop; or a prolongation of the thinking that went into the formation of my own verse." Yet he would not wish us to read his poetry through his criticism. The theoretical problem thus stated, like all important problems in literary criticism, would appear to be insoluble on the level of theory. But in practice it is of course a problem that can be effectively handled, at least in pragmatic fashion, by readers of good sense and judgment. I am reminded of Eliot's famous statement in *After Strange Gods* that "in one's prose reflexions one may be legitimately occupied with ideals, whereas in the writing of verse [and, I might add, in practical criticism] one can only deal with actuality."

The actuality of *The Waste Land*'s relation to its sources is partially revealed through what we know of the process of composition. The poem was largely written at Margate and Lausanne during the last three months of 1921, while Eliot was recuperating from a spiritual and physical breakdown. In a very real sense the writing of the poem was an act of reintegration, both of Eliot's personality and of his ten-year journey through the vortex of literary experiment. In retrospect, every aspect of his personal or literary experience available to us from the years 1920-1922 seems to point directly toward *The Waste Land*. For example, during 1921 and 1922 Eliot wrote a series of London letters for both the American and French audiences, published in *The Dial* and *Nouvelle Revue Française*: enter this material at any point and we are immediately confronted with another note to *The Waste Land*. In the London Letter to *The Dial* dated May 1921 Eliot closes with a gloomy note on the potential destruction of several Wren churches in the City of London, churches whose great beauty redeems "some vulgar street" or the "hideous banks and commercial houses." He contrasts by implication the frenzied business houses with the near-empty churches, "fallen into desuetude," and he concludes in this fashion:

"To one who, like the present writer, passes his days in this City of London (*quand'io sentii chiavar l'uscio di sotto*) the loss of these towers, to meet the eye down a grimy lane, and of these empty naves, to receive the solitary visitor at noon from the dust and tumult of Lombard Street, will be irreparable and unforgotten. A small pamphlet issued for the London County Council (Proposed Demolition of Nineteen City Churches: P. S. King & Son, Ltd., 2-4 Gt. Smith Street, Westminster, S. W. 1, 3s.6d. net) should be enough to persuade of what I have said."

This passage leads directly into two of the most moving and important sections of *The Waste Land*. The parenthetical reference to *Inferno* XXXIII shows that Eliot associated his own "imprisonment" in the City of London with Ugolino's imprisonment in the horrible tower. Ugolino, imprisoned and doomed to starve to death, heard the key turn below in the tower; the speaker at the end of *The Waste Land*, after reciting the ritual command to "sympathize," confesses:

> I have heard the key
> Turn in the door once and turn once only
> We think of the key, each in his prison
> Thinking of the key, each confirms a prison

In the note to this passage Eliot refers us to Canto XXXIII of the *Inferno*, quotes the same phrase used in the London Letter, and then connects it with one of F. H.

Bradley's remarks on the sealed-off nature of personal experience.

The other half of the passage from the London Letter leads directly to the vision of the City of London which occurs midway through *The Waste Land*:

"This music crept by me upon the waters"
And along the Strand, up Queen Victoria Street.
O City city, I can sometimes hear
Beside a public bar in Lower Thames Street,
The pleasant whining of a mandoline
And a clatter and a chatter from within
Where fishmen lounge at noon: where the walls
Of Magnus Martyr hold
Inexplicable splendour of Ionian white and gold.

Magnus Martyr, by the foot of London Bridge, was one of the Wren churches slated for destruction, and Eliot duly refers us in the notes to the pamphlet on *The Proposed Demolition of Nineteen City Churches*.

A similar pastiche of *données* for the poem can be found in the first paragraph of the London Letter for July 1921. London has been basking under a "hot rainless spring," Eliot tells his American audience; "a new form of influenza has been discovered, which leaves extreme dryness and a bitter taste in the mouth"; but paradoxically, the "blazing glare" has revealed for "the first time towers and steeples of an uncontaminated white." But in spite of the promise of the white towers, the dry spring has been accompanied by a cultural drought—the opera has deserted London, and Eliot compares himself by allusion to a victim of the Babylonian captivity: "They have forgotten thee, O Sion." In one way or another, all of these details later enter into the atmosphere and texture of *The Waste Land*, and the obscure allusion to Psalm 137 finds its counterpart at the beginning of Part III of the poem, where the speaker interjects a personal confession—"By the waters of Leman I sat down and wept."

All these details I have been recounting would seem to be perfect raw materials for some successor to John Livingston Lowes, interested in how the poem grew out of Eliot's reading and experience (perhaps the book will be called *The Road to Margate Sands*). But for the literary critic these details are at best peripheral, and at worst distracting; they belong to Eliot's biography, or to some investigation of the creative process, not to literary criticism as a study of form and context. They lie on the other side of the frontier Eliot was trying to establish in his 1956 lecture, and they make his fretful handling of the notes a good deal clearer. In effect, Eliot padded out the fundamental notes (the identifications of quotations and obvious allusions) with material from the private genesis of the poem, and therefore he well knew that he had invited—and even sanctioned—the investigation of another John Livingston Lowes.

But if Eliot's writings and reading of 1920 and 1921 are littered with the unassimilated raw materials of *The Waste Land*, which are not our immediate business, they also reveal "sources" or influences of a quite different kind, and these are very much the business of responsible criticism. Certain names run like *leitmotifs* through Eliot's writing and reading during the gestation period of *The Waste Land*, and they suggest the major forces which shaped his imagination at that time, and which—since they were shared in large measure by Ezra Pound—also shaped the joint process that turned a sequence of related poems into the highly articulated poem we now

16

know. These names are F. H. Bradley, Henry James, Joseph Conrad, Pound himself, Sir James Frazer, and James Joyce. In conclusion, I would like to comment briefly on some of these writers, since it seems to me that Eliot's responses to them offer the best chances for new perspectives on *The Waste Land* itself.

It is no accident that all but one of these writers worked in prose, and that the one poet—Ezra Pound—had impressed upon Eliot his famous motto, "Poetry should be at least as well written as prose"; by which Pound meant that most contemporary verse could not match the intensity and concentration found in the best fiction of Flaubert or Joyce. In a manner of speaking, *The Waste Land* brought to poetry many of the special achievements of the modern novel, both in its manipulation of narrative perspective and in its density of presentation. Although Eliot obviously did not feel that "the 'long poem' is a thing of the past," he did believe that "there must be more in it for the length than our grandparents seemed to demand; and for us, anything that can be said as well in prose can be said better in prose." Later, after his work on the *Quartets*, Eliot came to believe that the "long poem" needed a formula of alternating concentration and expansion, with passages of low intensity to set off the *symboliste* moments, but at the time of *The Waste Land* he clearly had in mind an ideal for the "long poem" not far from that of Edgar Allan Poe: an extended work of sustained lyrical intensity that could be absorbed at one sitting, or—to put it in spatial terms—an extended work that could still be grasped by the mind as a single Image, an emotional and intellectual complex apprehended in an instant of time (to paraphrase the Imagist manifesto). It is this ideal of compression that governed

17

all of Pound's suggestions for revision, and that lies be-
hind his final compliment: "The thing now runs from
'April . . .' to 'shantih' without a break. That is 19 pages,
and let us say the longest poem in the English langwidge.
Don't try to bust all records by prolonging it three pages
further." In effect, the tightening up of *The Waste Land*
was like Joyce's collapsing of *Stephen Hero* into the
"spots of time" that are *A Portrait of the Artist*: the aim
was a work of art which, in Conrad's motto, would carry
its justification for existence in every line.

In his "Preface to Modern Literature," first published
in May 1922, Eliot bracketed Joyce and Conrad as twin
masters of those modern fictional techniques, initially ex-
plored by Henry James, which are "struggling to digest
and express new objects, new groups of objects, new feel-
ings, new aspects" (he had made the same association
earlier in his Swinburne essay). Among the techniques
Eliot had in mind was clearly the manipulation of point-
of-view, a hallmark of recent experimental fiction. The
central *persona* of *The Waste Land* owes more to James's
"central consciousness" and Conrad's detached narrator
than to the various *personae* found in the poetry of Yeats
and Pound. The method that makes Tiresias, "although
a mere spectator and not indeed a 'character,' " the "most
important personage in the poem, uniting all the rest," is
a method Eliot learned by going to school to modern fic-
tion. He once thought of using a citation from Conrad's
"Heart of Darkness" ("The horror! the horror!") as an
epigraph for the poem, but the debt to Conrad's narrative
method is much more pervasive than any particular con-
nection with the desperate vision of Mr. Kurtz.

Two other pairings from Eliot's prose of this time
strike me as significant. One is the similarity in his dis-
cussions of Joyce and Frazer; the other is his constant

association of Henry James with F. H. Bradley. At the time when *The Waste Land* was written Frazer had just finished condensing the twelve volumes of *The Golden Bough* into one, and Eliot took this as an occasion to define the "profound influence" Frazer's anthropology had exercised upon his generation. In one essay he discussed Frazer under the startling rubric "A Vitalizing of the Classics," which might seem more appropriate to Joyce's *Ulysses*; and in *The Dial*'s London Letter dated September 1921 he discussed *The Golden Bough* in connection with Stravinsky's *Rites of Spring*.

"The effect was like *Ulysses* with illustrations by the best contemporary illustrator. . . . The spirit of the music was modern, and the spirit of the ballet was primitive ceremony. The Vegetation Rite upon which the ballet is founded remained, in spite of the music, a pageant of primitive culture. It was interesting to any one who had read *The Golden Bough* and similar works, but hardly more than interesting. In art there should be interpenetration and metamorphosis. Even *The Golden Bough* can be read in two ways: as a collection of entertaining myths, or as a revelation of that vanished mind of which our mind is a continuation. In everything in the *Sacre du Printemps*, except in the music, one missed the sense of the present. Whether Stravinsky's music be permanent or ephemeral I do not know; but it did seem to transform the rhythm of the steppes into the scream of the motor horn, the rattle of machinery, the grind of wheels, the beating of iron and steel, the roar of the underground railway, and the other barbaric cries of modern life; and to transform these despairing noises into music."

In short, Eliot found in Frazer and in Joyce the same "point of view," the same "vision"—the terms are his—which brought past and present into juxtaposition through myth and ritual. And it is surely this "vision," rather than any particular use of a mythological narrative, that Eliot had in mind when he wrote "*Ulysses*, Order, and Myth." It is a vision particularly congenial to the literary ideals of "Tradition and the Individual Talent," one which suggests that Eliot may have learned a great deal more from Joyce's handling of "Lycidas" and the death-by-water theme than he did from Joyce's use of the *Odyssey*. This is supported by the fact that the "Proteus" episode of *Ulysses*, which bears the closest analogies to *The Golden Bough*, passed through Eliot's hands in 1918, while he could not have seen the overall shape of Joyce's dependence on the *Odyssey* until after *The Waste Land* had been partially drafted.

I would like to ring one more change upon two names that echo through Eliot's prose of 1921-1922: F. H. Bradley (the subject of Eliot's doctoral thesis) and Henry James. Once again, as with Joyce and Frazer, it is the essential "vision" of these two men that Eliot finds compelling. He had long admired James, both as a master of psychological prose and as an example of the successful expatriate who never lost his peculiar qualities as an American writer. Like Pound, Eliot had contributed to the 1918 issue of *The Little Review* dedicated to James, and in his essay "Prediction in Regard to Three English Authors," first published in 1923, he linked James with Bradley as a "master of thought" as well as a "master of art." Eliot obviously saw in the novelist and the philosopher two congenial minds, each aware of "the disparity between possibility and fact," and Bradley's famous description of the plight of the individual personality (quoted in the notes to *The Waste Land*) applies equally well to the plight of one of Henry James's "poor gentlemen": "My external sensations are no less private to my-self than are my thoughts or my feelings. In either case my experience falls within my own circle, a circle closed on the outside; and, with all its elements alike, every sphere is opaque to the others which surround it. . . . the whole world for each is peculiar and private to that soul."

From first to last in Eliot's poetic career, from the undersea vision of Prufrock through the Hyacinth garden of *The Waste Land* to the rose garden of "Burnt Norton," it is a quintessentially Jamesian experience which lies at the heart of his work. The tragedy is that of one who can perceive but cannot act, who can understand and remember but cannot communicate. "I could not/ Speak, and my eyes failed, I was neither/ Living nor dead . . ./ Looking into the heart of light, the silence." At one time Eliot thought of titling the second part of *The Waste Land* "In the Cage," an obvious reference to James's novella where the little telegraph girl, shut into her wire cage, can only live vicariously through the communications that pass across her desk. She knows everything, and can act upon nothing: she is like Tiresias, who knows all, foresuffers all, and can prevent none of it.

This is the vision of personal isolation that Eliot shares with James, and that lies at the deepest reaches of all his works. And yet, like James, Eliot was possessed with the complementary "vision of an ideal society"; the result was an art aware at every turn of the "disparity between possibility and fact." In his later works Eliot does explore ways of breaking the "closed circle of consciousness," through discipline or through grace. But in *The Waste Land* the only consolation lies in memory and the vicarious ordering of past experience: "These fragments I have shored against my ruins." For those who need help in reaching the emotional center of *The Waste Land*, the surest guide lies not in Miss Jessie Weston's *From Ritual to Romance*, but in Henry James's "The Beast in the Jungle" and *The Sacred Fount*.

Hugh Kenner THE URBAN APOCALYPSE

THERE IS nothing so appeasing as a category; think how chaotic many eighteenth-century poems would seem if we did not know that we were supposed to call them Pindaric Odes. A name for the kind of poem *The Waste Land* is might have spared criticism much futile approximating. There used to be a kind of conducted tour, in which the student was bidden to observe how checkpoints would align if he closed one eye and sighted in the proper direction. This or that feature—the drowned man, the desert traveller, the unnerving woman—entered one or another thematic system, depending on the part of the terrain you were visiting, and the poem seemed a great feat of civil engineering. When the itinerary of one such tour was laid before Eliot, he remarked that he had not been conscious of being so ingenious, as though to say that the egg will exemplify mathematical shell-analysis of which the hen knows nothing. Yet the drafts, now that we have them, suggest a poem whose author might have described its plan. Though he seems to have found that poem impractical, it was from its wreckage that he sal-

23

vaged the poem we know, the first exemplar of a category that still has no name. To examine the drafts is to interrogate imperfect traces of a poem that was never achieved. Such an exercise needs no apology. *The Waste Land* is still a determinant of modernist consciousness, postmodernist also if it has come to that, and the profit of yet one more tour of speculation may be that we shall learn a little more about the history of our own minds.

To examine the drafts means for most of us to examine the reproductions in Valerie Eliot's 1971 facsimile edition. I have not been able to see the originals myself. Under even an unskilled eye, though, the reproductions suffice to dispel any notion of a longish poem called *The Waste Land* which its author wrote all at once and later shortened with help from a friend. Some of the handwriting is mature, some youthful—Valerie Eliot [130][1] dates three of the leaves "about 1914 or even earlier." The typescripts, moreover, have come from at least three typewriters. "Death by Water" and "What the Thunder Said" were both "typed with the violet ribbon used by Pound" [63, 83], hence in Paris after Eliot arrived there with holographs Pound declined to mark up [55].

More interesting, two different machines which I will call "A" and "B" were used for the rest of the copy. The title-page [3] and "The Fire Sermon" [23-47] display the elongated quotation marks and apostrophes of machine "A." But "The Burial of the Dead" [5-9], "A Game of Chess" [11-15], and the cancelled "Death of the Duchess" [105-107] exemplify machine "B," hence a different place and—we shall see—a different stratum of the poem. (As for the two remaining sheets of typescript, the

[1] All citations in square brackets refer to the facsimile edition of the original drafts.

24

shapes of lower-case "t's" and "f's" would assign "Exequy" [101] to the "A" family and "Song. For the Opherion" [99] to the "B," but these have no further importance for the argument.)

Comparison with typed correspondence would show where and when Eliot used machines "A" and "B." Pending such confirmation—or contradiction—there is reason to deduce that "A" was his London typewriter, "B" the one he used at Lausanne. If so, and I will explain later why I think so, he typed "The Fire Sermon" before leaving London, and took it with him to Switzerland, and its first state as printed in the facsimile edition represents the earliest continuous stretch of the poem.

A few dates next, to help bracket what may have been a catalyzing event. It is on 5 November 1919 [xvii-xviii] that we first hear Eliot hoping to get started on "a poem I have in mind." Six weeks later it is a long poem he has had on his mind "for a long time" [xviii], and nine months after that (20 September 1920) he is still longing for a little time to think about it [xx]. Then by 9 May 1921 something had happened: the poem was "partly on paper" [xxi]. The rest belongs to late 1921. In mid-October he went to Margate, where nothing connects with nothing; in mid-November to Lausanne. On 13 December, in Lausanne, he was "working on a poem" [xxii], and in Paris on his way back to London he laid before Pound the poem that he was later to tell John Quinn had been written "mostly when I was at Lausanne for treatment last winter" [xxii].

"Mostly" serves to exclude what he brought with him to Lausanne, notably whatever had been on paper since May. Now by some time in May 1921 Eliot had read Mark Van Doren's *John Dryden*, his review of which appeared in *The Times Literary Supplement* for June 9;[2] and not far into his first chapter we find Mark Van Doren explaining the late seventeenth-century vogue of Ovid, the poet "at once tender and mocking, at once flexible and hard, at once allusive and brisk, [who] taught Dryden his gait, and showed him how to turn all the sides of his mind to the light." Van Doren's explanation of this vogue is worth pondering: "For the first twenty years after the Restoration Dryden's London was to reproduce with a certain amount of accuracy the Rome of Ovid. With civil war just past and a commonwealth overthrown, with court and city beginning to realize their power, with peace prevailing and cynicism in fashionable morals rampant, with a foreign culture seeking the favor of patrons and wits, the new city did for a while bear a strange resemblance to the old Empire." (Third edition, 1946, p. 9.)

A war just past, a rampant cynicism, wits gone wild after continental novelty: we may guess how that could have sounded, in 1921, like contemporary London. Eliot's review does not cite the passage, confining itself as it does to advocacy of Dryden's verse. It does contain two suggestive statements: that "to enjoy Dryden means to pass beyond the limitations of the nineteenth century into a new freedom," and that the book under review is "a book which every practitioner of English verse should study."

Eliot's praise of Dryden in the 1920's, which extended even to calling one book of essays *Homage to John Dry-*

---

[2] The review is reprinted in *Selected Essays* as "John Dryden." From the fact [xviii] that on 5 November 1919 he was working on a review which *The Times Literary Supplement* published in its 13 November issue, we learn that its lead time for reviews was a week or less, so Eliot could have written his piece on Van Dor-

den, has not been assimilated by his commentators, for the good reason that until the *Waste Land* manuscripts were published in 1971 it was impossible to know what to make of it. Today, and especially from the first version of "The Fire Sermon," we can see how Dryden entered the conception of the unwritten poem, part of the rich amalgam that gathered in Eliot's mind in the months just before those decisive weeks in Lausanne.

To abridge much tedium of detail, we may summarize under two heads. The long poem was to be an urban poem, a London poem; and it was to be a poem of firm statements and strong lines, traceable to the decorums of urban satire.

Neither proposition need imply that Eliot was contemplating a radical change. He was always a city poet, not a country poet, his affinities rather with Baudelaire than with Wordsworth. And he was always quotable in the single line: "Let us go then, you and I." Still, he was changing. One novelty of the new poem was to be a new specificity: a public focus on his new environment, the City of London. His earlier poems immerse us in a city we cannot name. If we tend to suppose that Prufrock treads the streets of Boston, still his surname and his yellow fogs are from St. Louis, and the Paris of Laforgue has left its impress. But the crowd in the "Unreal City" flows over London Bridge, up the hill and down King William Street with St. Magnus Martyr and the Billingsgate Fish Market to its right, and the Thames Daughters' mortal places are on a map of the greater London area: Highbury, Richmond, Kew, Moorgate. One passage, drafted amid swarms of variants [37], typed into "The

---

en's *Dryden* as late as, say, June 1. I wish I knew how much earlier he was reading in the book, but let us guess several weeks. Its American copyright date is 1920.

Fire Sermon" and finally cancelled, confronted the per-
sonified City:

> London, the swarming life you kill and breed,
> Huddled between the concrete and the sky,
> Responsive to the momentary need,
> Vibrates unconscious to its formal destiny,
>
> Knowing neither how to think, nor how to feel,
> But lives in the awareness of the observing eye.
> Phantasmal gnomes, burrowing in brick and stone and
>   steel!
> Some minds, aberrant from the normal equipoise
> (London, your people is bound upon the wheel!)
> Record the movements of these pavement toys
> And trace the cryptogram that may be curled
> Within the faint perceptions of the noise
> Of the movement, and the lights!
>
> Not here, O Glaucon, but in another world. [31, 43]

Though it drew a rude marginal expletive from Pound,
this seems to have been meant for a focal passage, sug-
gesting in conjunction with other details that the mytho-
logical unity Eliot's notes encourage us to find in the final
poem was at one time a geographical unity. (Another
passage commencing "O City, City," later used as the
basis of lines 259-65, was drafted on the same sheet
[37].) London, killing and breeding, Eliot seems to have
intuited as a sort of presiding personage, the original
Fisher King as well as the original Waste Land, resem-
bling Augustine's Carthage as Dryden's London had re-
sembled Ovid's Rome.

The passage commences with a four-line stanza, set off
by a space and rhymed *a b a b*, a stanza that just a little
later in "The Fire Sermon" was repeated seventeen more

times. This is an uncommon stanza, recognizable to most modern ears because Gray used it in his *Elegy*. Mark Van Doren (pp. 82-84) has something to say about its history, and about Dryden's persisting fascination with its "leisurely authority." Before Dryden, Spenser, Davies, Donne, and Ben Jonson had used it, and D'Avenant in *Gondibert*. Most pertinently, it is the stanza of *Annus Mirabilis*, which just here in "The Fire Sermon" it seems calculated to echo.

Annus Mirabilis (as Van Doren notes) was dedicated "To the Metropolis of Great Britain, the Most Renown'd and Late Flourishing City of London." Dryden commenced his preface with the supposition that he might be "the first who ever presented a work of this nature to the metropolis of any nation," a boldness he justifies by suggesting that no city ever so much deserved such praise. Other cities, he says, have won their fame "by cheaper trials than an expensive, tho' necessary war, a consuming pestilence, and a more consuming fire." The last twelve stanzas of *Annus Mirabilis* are singled out by Van Doren. They "pile themselves up," he says (p. 111), "like the Theban stones that obeyed Amphion's lyre," to prophesy London's illimitable future:

298

... The silver Thames, her own domestic flood,
    Shall bear her vessels like a sweeping train;
    And often wind (as of his mistress proud)
    With longing eyes to meet her face again.

299

The wealthy Tagus, and the wealthier Rhine,
    The glory of their towns no more shall boast;
    And Seine, that would with Belgian rivers join,
    Shall find her luster stain'd, and traffic lost.

300
The vent'rous merchant, who design'd more far,
  And touches on this hospitable shore,
Charm'd with the splendor of this northern star,
  Shall here unlade him, and depart no more. . . .

Such was the prospect before London in 1666. By
1921, having undergone yet one more "expensive, tho'
necessary war," and one more "consuming pestilence"
which figures in demographic history as the great influ-
enza epidemic, it was playing host to such ambivalently
vent'rous merchants as Mr. Eugenides, "unshaven, with
a pocket full of currants," and seemed ripe for a Fire Ser-
mon if not for a fire.

Unreal City [wrote Eliot] I have seen and see
Under the brown fog of your winter noon
Mr. Eugenides, the Smyrna merchant . . . [31]

and he followed this with the apostrophe to London that
commences in the stanza of *Annus Mirabilis*, the "heroic
stanza," alternately rhymed, which Dryden was to call
"more noble, and of greater dignity, both for the sound
and number, than any other verse in use amongst us."

It specifies in what respect the City is Unreal: unreal
the way sensate accretions are unreal for Plato, to whose
Republic the line about Glaucon directs us [127-28]. Its
whole life has been levelled down to the plane of sensa-
tion. To this, to the likes of Mr. Eugenides, to a life of
"phantasmal gnomes" and "pavement toys," has the Lon-
don of Dryden's magniloquent prophecy come: that
seems to be the tacit burden of these details, and, after a
few lines irregularly rhymed, Eliot wrote seventeen more
heroic stanzas, presenting in Dryden's form though not
his diction the movements of the typist and the youth with

the spotted face who enact an unreal automation of Love itself [31-35, 43-47].

That passage, Tiresias' vision, as we know from the manuscripts, was all in the *Annus Mirabilis* stanza once, and the fine laconic gravity of its present state was achieved by ruthless deletion that cut through quatrains and amalgamated their details. By then the poem's coordinates had so shifted that a tacit allusion to Dryden no longer mattered, and Eliot made no effort to preserve the stanzas' identity. He had dwelt, in the longest portion that got deleted, on the uncivil habits of the young man. A quatrain ran

> —Bestows one final patronizing kiss,
> And gropes his way, finding the stairs unlit;
> And at the corner where the stable is,
> Delays only to urinate, and spit.

Pound [47] called the last two lines "over the mark," as they were. As to why Eliot first included them, we may learn less from dwelling on what is called his social snobbery than from weighing his statement that the neglect of Dryden is "not due to the fact that his work is not poetry, but to a prejudice that the material, the feelings out of which he built is not poetic." The urination and the spitting near the stable, like other constellations of low detail—

> He munches with the same persistent stare,
> He knows his way with women and that's that!
> Impertinently tipping back his chair
> And dropping cigarette ash on the mat   [45]

—seem meant to affirm, with a confidence perhaps enforced by the reading [xx] of the latter parts of *Ulysses* in typescript, that material of that order will make poetry,

31

and in the way Dryden made poetry, by making plain statements. "When Dryden became fired," says Van Doren, "he only wrote more plainly. . . . His passion was the passion of assurance. His great love was the love of speaking fully and with finality." Eliot's Tiresias too spoke that way, as well in the strongest parts of the typist passage as in the ones reconsideration discarded.

> She turns and looks a moment in the glass,
> Hardly aware of her departed lover;
> Her brain allows one half-formed thought to pass:
> 'Well now that's done: and I'm glad it's over.'

This is without doubt the poetry of plain statement, and when Pound helped it toward the form in which we know it he simply made it plainer. Eliot had written, "Across her brain one half-formed thought may pass," and Pound's thick pencil jabbed at the word "may" and scribbled in the margin, "make up yr. mind." The rest of his comment is almost a free-verse stanza:

> you Tiresias
> if you know
> know damn well
> or
> else you
> dont.   [47]

This brings us around to the suggestive fact that collaborative revision was possible at all. It was possible because the main criteria Eliot's verse implied were as easy to formulate as they were difficult to sustain. They were the criteria of the strong line, the ample unfilagreed statement, its normative unit the end-stopped pentameter coincident with a closed syntactic member.

The time is now propitious, as he guesses,
The meal is ended, she is bored and tired;
Endeavours to engage her in caresses,
Which still are unreproved, if undesired.

Such a quatrain proclaims its Restoration ancestry: straightforward syntax, with a high proportion of principal to dependent clauses; Latin precision—"propitious," "endeavours"—lending overtones of wit to its completion of native monosyllables; and the neat closing antithesis, "unreproved, if undesired," establishing a viewpoint which is not that of the innocent eye but that of the Lockean judgment, making distinctions. "Carbuncular," in what is perhaps the most famous line in the passage, is another weightily felicitous Latinism: "He, the young man carbuncular, arrives"; and with still more felicitous wit it follows its noun in the manner of a French adjective, rather a taxonomy than an epithet.

But such verse, so sparse, so centered on its affirmations, cannot justify itself by its wit or its local accuracy, only by a certain authority which is part of what Eliot meant by "impersonality," which may correspond to what is called "sincerity" in the poet, but of which his sincerity is by no means the guarantee. Of verses composed by these canons of statement, Dr. Johnson once remarked that the difficulty was not to make them but to know when you had made good ones. Johnson often helped other poets who were in that difficulty. We learn from Boswell of lines he supplied for Goldsmith, and if we had the manuscript we might find in it lines he deleted, the readiest way to improve imperfect Augustan verse being to take things out. Sense tends to collect itself into metrical units, and build by accumulation; passage-structure is paratactic, and omissions do not show.

So like a pair of bohemian Augustans, Pound and Eliot that winter in Paris worked over passages that recapitulated the literary procedures of a period. Pound mostly removed things; or else he fussed so much at a quatrain's details that Eliot himself removed it rather than recast. The heroic stanzas which were introduced by an echo of Dryden's apostrophe to London concluded with a parodic allusion to Goldsmith ("When lovely woman stoops to folly"). Goldsmith survived the revision but all identifiable trace of Dryden vanished, the heroic stanzas having become an irregularly rhymed sequence of "strong lines." Also gone was the long opening of "The Fire Sermon," which had imitated Pope. Of this there was nothing left at all, not a line, and there was no way to tell that the whole central section of Eliot's long poem had moved through modes of Augustan imitation.

The Popish passage deserves a moment's attention. At the root of its troubles lay Eliot's deficient grasp of Pope, concerning whom, in the absence of any critic to do what Mark Van Doren had done for Dryden, he was damnably at the mercy of *idées reçues*. Judging (as we learn from his *Times Literary Supplement* leader on Dryden) that Pope's way was to trivialize and to belittle, he adopted what he took to be Pope's idiom for a character who invited belittling, the pretentious lady taking tea in bed.

> Admonished by the sun's declining ray,
> And swift approaches of the thievish day,
> The white-armed Fresca blinks, and yawns, and gapes,
> Aroused by dreams of loves and pleasant rapes.
> Electric summons of the busy bell
> Brings brisk Amanda to destroy the spell;
> With coarsened hand, and hard plebeian tread,
> Who draws the curtain round the lacquered bed,

> Depositing thereby a polished tray
> Of soothing chocolate, or stimulating tea.   [23]

The day is thievish, the rapes are pleasant, the summons
(in the best touch in the passage) electric, the bell busy,
Amanda brisk, the bed lacquered, the tea stimulating;
deprived of their adjectives, none of the perceptions in
these ten lines is of interest, their author having supposed
Pope to consist of sequential clichés redeemed by adjecti-
val justness. Pound noted on the carbon copy that the
couplets (which Eliot was to recall thinking excellent)
were "too loose" ("rhyme drags it out to diffuseness"),
and on the ribbon copy, after pausing over minute im-
provements, he slashed out the whole seventy lines. What
was built on adjectives was built on sand.

London, perceived through various Augustan modes:
that was "The Fire Sermon" originally. It might have
been entitled *London: a Poem*, or even *The Vanity of
Human Wishes*. If work on this section was indeed pre-
cipitated by the reading of Mark Van Doren's book about
Dryden, it may well contain what had gotten on paper
by May. Anyhow, it preceded Lausanne, and went there
in Eliot's luggage: two typed copies, original and carbon,
transcribed on the "A" machine. The rest of the poem
seems to have been planned around it, guided by the
norms and decorums of an Augustan view of history.
When the plan faltered and changed, the historical norms
changed too. Still, we can reconstruct them.

Eras and cultures resemble one another, and from their
resemblance we can collect a normative sense of what it
can mean to live in a civilization. The English Augustans
had been encouraged by points of correspondence be-
tween their London and the Rome of Augustus. Eliot's
parallel is between Augustan London and modern, and it

does not hearten. It signifies a relapse into habit. History, Eliot had written in 1919, "gives when our attention is distracted." By this he appears to mean something like what Wyndham Lewis meant in the 1917 "Inferior Religions," an essay Eliot admired: that to fall into the rhythms of an archetype, into "the habit-world or system of a successful personality," is to be guilty of inattention. "A comic type is a failure of a considerable energy," Lewis had written, "an imitation and standardizing of self." Such beings are "illusions hugged and lived in, little dead totems." That elucidates one of Eliot's couplets about the fashionable lady, that

> Women grown intellectual grow dull
> And lose the mother wit of natural trull,   [27]

and such an image as "pavement toys," and such a passage as the one about how things are in Hampstead, which he typed in Lausanne and may have composed just after he got there, the urban satirist's impulse still upon him:

> The inhabitants of Hampstead have silk hats
> On Sunday afternoon go out to tea
> On Saturday have tennis on the lawn, and tea
> On Monday to the city, and then tea.
> They know what they are to feel and what to think,
> They know it with their morning printer's ink
> They have another Sunday when the last is gone
> They know what to think and what to feel
> The inhabitants of Hampstead are bound forever on
>   the wheel.   [105]

And it illuminates his use of historical parallels. In *Annus Mirabilis* Dryden, meaning to enhance the recent war with the Dutch, compares it to the Second Punic War. In

36

The Waste Land Eliot introduces an ex-sailor who has fought in some analogue of the First Punic War—"You who were with me in the ships at Mylae!"—by way of suggesting that the same dreary wars recur as the wheel revolves. His point seems not to be, what used to be often alleged, that the present is tediously inferior to the past: rather that the present is inferior to its own best potential insofar as it courts resemblance to the past. Tradition, with the whole past of Europe in its bones, ought to be engaged on something new.

The Conrad epigraph Eliot later proposed enforces this theme of paralyzing reenactment: "Did he live his life again in every detail of desire, temptation and surrender during that supreme moment of complete knowledge?" For if history gives when our attention is distracted, so does personal circumstance, and if London had become a kind of jumbled quotation of former cities, he himself too in his unfortunate marriage had become something like a quotation: a character in an over-familiar play, which sometimes seemed to be *The Duchess of Malfi* and sometimes a French farce. "The Death of the Duchess" [105-107] moves between Hampstead farce and Websterian domesticity. Eliot's decision not to include it in his long poem seems to have come early; he gutted it for details—the game of chess, the knock upon the door—to use in the multi-parted work he now thought of calling *He Do the Police in Different Voices.*

This title, a whimsical comment on the poem's polyphony, would have also served to imply that the police news embodied the nineteenth-century's poetic of fact; and would have invoked too at the poem's threshold, for readers who caught the allusion [125] to *Our Mutual Friend,* the Dickens whose art is inseparable from London and whose genre is the urban satirist's as it was Hogarth's and Dryden's.

37

So across a sheet headed "The Burial of the Dead," we find typed *He Do the Police in Different Voices: Part I.* This comprehensive heading is misaligned with the rest of the page, which suggests a second, probably later, insertion of paper into machine [4]. At the head of Part II, however, the Dickens title sits on the page as though it had been meant to be there from the start. We may guess that Eliot had typed at least the first page of Part I before he thought of the overall title. His faith in it seems to have wavered. He never crossed it out. On the other hand he did not write or type it on any of the extant copies of Parts III, IV, and V. Only some weeks later did the long poem acquire a title it could live with.

So we have Eliot now in Lausanne, transcribing on the "B" typewriter what he meant for semi-final versions of Parts I and II. Part I commenced with a panorama of his own recent life: an undergraduate spree in Cambridge (Mass.), café talk in Munich, the morning crowd in London. All this was headed "The Burial of the Dead," a less mystifying title when the sequence of personal pasts was more prominent than it later became.

The sequence brings him to the Unreal City, where Mme. Sosostris reads cards, and where a section title, "In the Cage," invites us to see the woman in the ornate chair and the woman in the pub who knows so much about Lil and Albert as lurid extrapolations from an 1890 tale by Henry James.[3] Mme. Sosostris' cards may remind us of the riddling leaves of the Sibyl of Cumae in the sixth book

[3] Mrs. Eliot's note connects this title, which Eliot later cancelled, with the Sibyl of *The Waste Land*'s epigraph, hanging "in a cage" (*in ampulla*). But "cage," though the Loeb translator uses it, is a doubtful rendition of "ampulla" (bottle, jar); moreover it remains to be demonstrated that Eliot at that time had any notion of affixing the quotation from Petronius without which an allusion to the decrepit Sibyl would be impenetrable.

of the *Aeneid*, whose injunction to Aeneas, when he wanted to visit the Underworld, required him not only to locate the golden bough but to perform for a drowned companion the rite of the burial of the dead. As we brood on the first parts of the poem in their first form, points of contact with the *Aeneid* multiply: Carthage and the Punic Wars Dido prophesied, the drowned sailor, the Sibyl and her enigmas, the horn and ivory gates [31: later cancelled], even such a detail as the word "laquearia" (*Aen*. I: 726), which hints that the woman in the chair, rendered in the dead luxurious diction of Huysmans or the Mallarmé of *Hérodiade*,[4] is a kind of Dido, to interfere with the traveller's proper destiny. That would have been one way to imagine Vivien Eliot, whose "Yes & wonderful wonderful" written up the margin of a passage [13] projected from the hell she and Tom inhabited is quite the most unnerving detail in these fifty-four leaves of manuscript.

Multum ille et terris jactatus et alto: Eliot, much impressed by Joyce's use of Homer, may well have had in

---

[4] Compare:

> Et sur les incarnats, grand ouvert, ce vitrail.
>
> La chambre singulière en un cadre, attirail
> De siècle belliqueux, orfèvrerie éteinte,
> A le neigeux jadis pour ancienne teinte,
> Et sa tapisserie, au lustre nacré, plis
> Inutiles avec les yeux ensevelis
> De sibylles offrant leur ongle vieil aux Mages.
> Une d'elles, avec un passé de ramages
> Sur ma robe blanchie en l'ivoire fermé
> Au ciel d'oiseaux parmi l'argent noir parsemé,
> Semble, de vols partir costumée et fantôme,
> Un arôme qui porte, o rôses! un arôme,
> Loin du lit vide qu'un cierge soufflé cachait,
> Un arôme d'ors froids rôdant sur le sachet. . . .
> —*Hérodiade*, I

mind at one time a kind of modern *Aeneid*, the hero crossing seas to pursue his destiny, detained by one woman and prophesied to by another, and encountering visions of the past and the future, all culminated in a city both founded and yet to be founded, unreal and oppressively real, the Rome through whose past Dryden saw London's future.

In "The Fire Sermon"—which he neglected to number "Part III" though he must have been counting it when he headed "Death by Water" "Part IV"—London travesties Dryden's vatic prediction. Were Eliot's readers meant to bridge an ellipse by thinking of Dryden as a British Anchises, and the finale to *Annus Mirabilis* as analogous to the famous evocation of Rome's future (*Aen.* VI: 847-53) that Aeneas heard from his dead father's lips in the Underworld? We can hardly expect to know. The "Fire Sermon" typescript apparently preceded such formal decisions as shaped Parts I and II, and needed more work to clarify its status. On the back of its first leaf [25] Eliot drafted a passage in which the last fingers of leaf clutch the river's wet bank. Conceivably one thing that prompted this was Vergil's account of the unburied dead thronging the bank of Acheron,

> Quam multa in silvis autumni frigore primo
> Lapsa cadunt folia   (*Aen.* VI: 309-310)

In the final version of the poem, "The Fire Sermon" opens with this passage. On the back of its third leaf he drafted lines to be inserted into the Fresca passage, aligning her with Venus Anadyomene and recalling how

> To Aeneas, in an unfamiliar place,
> Appeared his mother, with an altered face,
> He knew the goddess by her smooth celestial
>   pace.   [29]

That would have helped bring Fresca into the myth; but the Fresca passage was cancelled.[5]

In Part IV ("Death by Water") we are still in the Underworld. The speaker is a dead sailor from New England recounting how they ran into an iceberg. By the time he drafted this, we may speculate, Eliot was losing his grip on the poem he had set out to write. The original "Death by Water" [55-61] has trouble with idiom, trouble with rhythm, trouble with tone, and we note mechanical efforts to link it with the rest of the poem by recalling Dante's Ulysses and working in bits of diction from Tennyson's. A typewriter being for some reason inaccessible, Eliot had made a holograph fair copy, which Pound [55] declined to "attack" until he got a typescript. The passage was accordingly typed on Pound's machine, and its imperfections attacked to such effect that the entire narrative portion, eighty-two lines, simply vanished, leaving only ten appended lines about Phlebas the Phoenician, Englished from a French poem ("Dans le Restaurant") that had been published in the *Little Review* three years before.

The decision to scrap the rest was unarguably correct, as much so as the decision to retain "What the Thunder Said" intact, little though that had to do with what seems

[5] That these passages were drafted in Lausanne seems a reasonable assumption. After the conference with Pound in Paris, the Fresca passage was marked for deletion, so there would have been no point writing an insert for it. On the other hand, you do not use the back of your typescript for drafts unless you have decided the typescript will have to be done over, so Eliot's decision that Part III needed more work seems to have preceded Pound's major surgery. My guess is that he was trying to incorporate an *Aeneid* parallel he had decided on since he first wrote it. Vivien Eliot was later to insert a version of "Fresca" into a *Criterion* article [127]. The editor [23] calls this an earlier draft, but it reads to me like a later one. Eliot hated to throw things away altogether.

to have been the poem's working plan. "What the Thunder Said" was virtually a piece of automatic writing. Eliot more than once testified that he wrote it almost at a sitting, apparently so late in his stay at Lausanne that he did not have time to make a fair copy, and the rapid handwriting of the holograph [71-81] bears him out. False starts and second thoughts are few, and later retouching was insignificant. One of the first thoughts is arresting: the fourth line from the end ran, "These fragments I have spelt into my ruins," to imply that the protagonist has visited the Sibyl of Vergil, whose oracles, like those of Mme. Sosostris, were fragmentary and shuffled by the winds. Above "spelt into" Eliot wrote "shored against," but he did not cross out the earlier phrase and opted for "shored" only when he made the typescript.[6]

Some of the materials for these pages had been on Eliot's mind many years; the opening, and the apocalyptic passage with the bats and the whisper-music and the towers upside-down in air, reproduce and improve scraps of verse [109, 113] that Valerie Eliot dates from the handwriting "1914 or even earlier" [130]. For at least seven years, it would seem, an urban apocalypse had haunted Eliot's imagination, its first version tied to such images of walking through a city as we find in "Rhapsody on a Windy Night."

> So through the evening, through the violet air
> One tortured meditation dragged me on
> Concatenated words from which the sense
>   seemed gone—

[6] One of several reasons for rejecting the suggestion [83] that Pound may have done the typing. In particular, his mannerism of hitting the space-bar twice is nowhere visible. And the spelling of "Hieronymo" has been corrected and the italicization of the Sanskrit regularized—not the sort of detail Pound took care over.

The as-if-senseless words on this early page [113] include a draft of the familiar passage that begins "A woman drew her long black hair out tight." There was also a Prufrockian bit, not later used, in which a man like Lazarus declines to return to life.

In the remarkable upwelling of language to which the holograph draft of Part v is testimony, this vein of material virtually took possession of the poem. The motifs familiar from commentaries appeared: the nightmare journey, the Chapel, the Quester, the Grail Legend, the Fisher King. Later, the notes would encourage us to perceive their applicability to what revision had left of the earlier sections, and luckily one enigmatic passage in Section I, with "a heap of broken images" and a red rock, would give the opening of the poem the look of having foreseen its closing.

For it is difficult to believe that anyone who saw only the first four parts in their original form would believe that "the plan and a good deal of the incidental symbolism" were suggested by Jessie Weston's book on the Grail Legend, or that *The Golden Bough* (Frazer's, not Vergil's) had much pertinence. If we were asked to nominate a controlling scheme, we might more plausibly guess that the pages before us had something to do with the *Aeneid*, notably its sixth book. If we guessed, from Mme. Sosostris, that the Sibyl was present, we should surely connect her with the Sibyl of Vergil, dealing out her fragments of prophecy (*Aen.* III, 444), than with the Sibyl of Petronius, withered and longing to die. The Sibyl of Petronius entered the explicit scheme only via an epigraph that was added later than anything recorded in the manuscripts.

The decision to entitle the poem *The Waste Land* seems also to have come late. Its only occurrence in the manuscripts is on a title-page with the Conrad epigraph, typed neither on the "B" typewriter we have assigned to Lausanne nor on the one with Pound's violet ribbon that was used in Paris, but on the "A" machine, the one on which "The Fire Sermon" was transcribed. And it seems doubtful that the title-page and "The Fire Sermon" were typed at the same sitting. We have seen Pound working over the "Fire Sermon" typescript. On the other hand, his comment on the Conrad citation (D. D. Paige ed., *The Letters of Ezra Pound*, No. 181) implies that he had not seen it before, one indication that this title-page, and incidentally this title, was not part of what he saw in Paris.

This letter was written on 24 January 1921,[7] some time after Eliot's return to London, and clearly pertains to a fresh typescript, received in the mail, one that took nineteen pages to run "from 'April . . .' to 'shantih' without a break." Three short pieces—probably "Song," "Exequy," and "Dirge"—were tacked on at the end, but on Pound's advice Eliot removed them without protest.

There can be no doubt that the poem was retyped. Nineteen pages seems a trustworthy figure—Pound used it again in his 21 February letter to John Quinn—and there is no plausible way to extract it from the existing

---

[7] Paige antedates it by a month, which makes the whole chronology impossible. Pound typed "24 Saturnus, An 1," amusing himself with a calendar that terminated the Christian Era at midnight, 29/30 October 1921, when Joyce completed *Ulysses*, and dating subsequent events p.s.U., i.e. *post scriptum Ulixi*. See Letter No. 185, undated letters from Pound to Margaret Anderson at the University of Wisconsin, Milwaukee, and the calendar itself in *The Little Review*, Spring 1922, p. 2 and note, p. 40. October 30 (Pound's birthday) was designated Feast of Zagreus, October 31 Feast of Pan, and the year commenced with Hephaistos (November, old style). December was Zeus and Saturnus was January.

typed pages. Of these, Parts I, II, and V, plus a page for Phlebas, total only ten sheets, leaving nearly half the total for the recast Fire Sermon, which is absurd.

So there was a new typescript, probably double-spaced, the theme of the published correspondence between the two poets, and vanished now. And it is highly probable that the title-page now among the manuscripts was part of it. Since the scrupulous Eliot did not include this typescript among the manuscript materials he sent to Quinn on 23 October 1922 [xxix], we may entertain the probability that it was the emergency copy he had already sent Quinn on July 19 [xxiii] for transmittal to Horace Liveright when the book contract was being negotiated. From the fact that Quinn only gleaned the title of the book from a postscript of Pound's, we infer that the copy he was sent in July lacked a title-page; the most plausible guess is that Eliot was still looking for a new epigraph, and had meanwhile removed the title-page from the typescript. The epigraph would have gone to Liveright later, along with the notes, and the rejected title-page—the one we have—was attached to the other *brouillons* of the poem when they went off to Quinn in October.

It is apparently all that survives of that nineteen-page typescript, and since it was typed on the "A" machine the probability grows very high that the "A" machine was Eliot's London typewriter. And since "The Fire Sermon" was typed on the "A" machine it was typed in London, one ground for inferring that it was one of the earliest parts of the poem. Undisclosed facts that may bring down this card-house of inference are unlikely to make the story of the poem's composition any simpler.

So it would have been about mid-January 1922, in London, that *The Waste Land* received its final form, and likely its title too. The state of the manuscripts Eliot had

45

unpacked after his return from the continent may be readily summarized. "The Burial of the Dead" had lost its Cambridge opening but was otherwise lightly annotated. "A Game of Chess" had had its opening heavily worked over by Pound, to tighten the meter, and Vivien Eliot had supplied a few suggestions for improving the pub dialogue. "The Fire Sermon" was a shambles; it needed much work. "Death by Water" had been cut back to ten lines. "What the Thunder Said" was "OK."

Pondering these materials, Eliot perceived where the poem's center of gravity now lay. Its center was no longer the urban panorama refracted through Augustan styles. That had gone with the dismemberment of Part III. Its center had become the urban apocalypse, the great City dissolved into a desert where voices sang from exhausted wells, and the Journey that had been implicit from the moment he opened the poem in Cambridge and made its course swing via Munich to London had become a journey through the Waste Land. Reworking Part III, and retyping the other parts with revisions of detail, he achieved the visionary unity that has fascinated two generations of readers. He then went to bed with the flu, "excessively depressed." (Pound *Letters*, appendix to No. 181.)

He was anxious. He thought of deleting Phlebas, and was told that the poem needed Phlebas "ABsolootly." "The card pack introduces him, the drowned phoen. sailor." He thought of using "Gerontion" as a prelude, and was told not to. "One don't miss it *at* all as the thing now stands." (Pound *Letters*, No. 182.) What seems to have bothered him was the loss of a schema. "Gerontion" would have made up for that lack by turning the whole thing into "thoughts of a dry brain in a dry season." Later the long note about Tiresias attempted the same strategy:

46

"What Tiresias *sees,* in fact, is the substance of the poem." The lost schema, if we have guessed about it correctly, had originated in a preoccupation with Dryden as the poem grew outward from "The Fire Sermon." If Vergil had once sponsored the protagonist's journey as Homer sponsors the wanderings of Leopold Bloom, Vergil was pertinent to a poem prompted by Vergil's major English translator, John Dryden. Ovid, who supplied Tiresias and Philomel, and told (*Metam.* xiv) the story of the Sibyl's terrible longevity which may underlie the line about fear in a handful of dust, was a favorite of Dryden's, and (on Mark Van Doren's showing) pertinent to Dryden's London and Eliot's. Wren's churches, notably Magnus Martyr, were built after the fire *Annus Mirabilis* celebrates, which is one reason Eliot works Magnus Martyr into his Fire Sermon. And in disposing ornate diction across the grid of a very tame pentameter, Eliot's original draft of the opening of Part ii had rewritten in the manner of French decadence a Shakespearean passage (". . . like a burnished throne") that Dryden had rewritten before him in a diction schooled by his own time's French decorum. No classroom exercise is more ritualized than the comparison of *Antony and Cleopatra* and *All for Love.*

But the center from which such details radiate had been removed from the poem. What survived was a form with no form, and a genre with no name. Years later, on the principle that a form is anything done twice, Eliot reproduced the structural contours of *The Waste Land* exactly, though more briefly, in *Burnt Norton,* and later still three more times, to make the *Quartets,* the title of which points to a decision that such a form might have analogies with music. That was *post facto.* In 1922, deciding somewhat reluctantly that the poem called *The*

Waste Land was finished, he was assenting to a critical judgment, Pound's and his own, concerning which parts were alive in a sheaf of pages he had written. Two years afterward, in "The Function of Criticism," he averted to "the capital importance of criticism in the work of creation itself," and suggested that "the larger part of the labour of an author in composing his work is critical labour; the labour of sifting, combining, constructing, expunging, correcting, testing." He called it "this frightful toil," and distinguished it from obedience to the Inner Voice. "The critical activity finds its highest, its true fulfilment in a kind of union with creation in the labour of the artist." (*Selected Essays*, "The Function of Criticism," IV.)

For it does no discredit to *The Waste Land* to learn that it was not striving from the first to become the poem it became: that it was not conceived as we have it before it was written, but reconceived from the wreckage of a different conception. Eliot saw its possibilities in London, in January 1922, with the mangled drafts before him: that was a great feat of creative insight.

In Paris he and Pound had worked on the poem page by page, piecemeal, not trying to salvage a structure but to reclaim the authentic lines and passages from the contrived. Contrivance had been guided by various neo-classic formalities, which tended to dispose the verse in single lines whose sense could survive the deletion of their neighbors.

When they had finished, and Eliot had rewritten the central section, the poem ran, in Pound's words, "from 'April . . .' to 'shantih' without a break." This is true if your criterion for absence of breaks is Symbolist, not neo-classical. Working over the text as they did, shaking out ashes from amid the glowing coals, leaving the luminous bits to discover their own unexpected affinities, they nearly recapitulated the history of Symbolism, a poetic that systematized the mutual affinities of details neo-classic canons had guided. Eliot in his *Times Literary Supplement* review had paid Dryden the unexpected compliment, that in being prizeworthy for what he had made of his material he resembled Mallarmé. It was something akin to Mallarmé, finally, that his own effort to assimilate Dryden came to resemble: the ornate *Hérodiade*, or the strange visions ("Une dentelle s'abolit . . .") of unpeopled rooms where detail strains toward detail and we cannot feel sure what the rhetoric portends.

AFTERWORD

I am grateful to Professor Ralph Rader, who heard the English Institute version of this essay, for some confirming suggestions I have worked into the present revision.

And a letter from Prof. Stanley Sultan, received when these pages were in proof, removes any doubt that the "A" typewriter was Eliot's London machine. He used it to address the packet of *Waste Land* MSS to John Quinn. The label bears the typed return address, "From T. S. Eliot, 9, Clarence Gate Gardens, London N. W. 1." and is postmarked "London, October 23 1922." It is reproduced opposite p. 11 of the New York Public Library's 1968 catalogue of its John Quinn Exhibition. Professor Sultan also points to the absence of a part number on the draft of "The Fire Sermon" as confirming evidence that it antedates any decision about the amount of material that should precede it.

With this essay in proof the mail brings *Mosaic* VI-1, where I find that Grover Smith ("The Making of *The Waste Land*," pp. 127-141) has also read the riddle of the typewriters and reached virtually identical conclusions about the sequence of the drafts. Though our notions of what went into the poem differ greatly, I am delighted to have his confirmation of the chronology.

Richard Ellmann

THE FIRST *WASTE LAND*

LLOYDS' most famous bank clerk revalued the poetic currency fifty years ago. As Joyce said, *The Waste Land* ended the idea of poetry for ladies. Whether admired or detested, it became, like *Lyrical Ballads* in 1798, a traffic signal. Hart Crane's letters, for instance, testify to his prompt recognition that from that time forward his work must be to outflank Eliot's poem. Today footnotes do their worst to transform innovations into inevitabilities. After a thousand explanations, *The Waste Land* is no longer a puzzle poem, except for the puzzle of choosing among the various solutions. To be penetrable is not, however, to be predictable. The sweep and strangeness with which Eliot delineated despair resist temptations to patronize Old Possum as old hat. Particular discontinuities continue to surprise even if the idea of discontinuous form—to which Eliot never quite subscribed and which he was to forsake—is now almost as familiar as its sober counterpart. The compound of regular verse and *vers libre* still wears some of the effrontery with which in 1922 it flouted both schools. The poem retains the air of a splendid feat.

51

Eliot himself was inclined to poohpooh its grandeur. His chiseled comment, which F. O. Matthiessen quotes, disclaimed any intention of expressing "the disillusionment of a generation," and said that he did not like the word "generation" or have a plan to endorse anyone's "illusion of disillusion." To Theodore Spencer he remarked in humbler mood, "Various critics have done me the honour to interpret the poem in terms of criticism of the contemporary world, have considered it, indeed, as an important bit of social criticism. To me it was only the relief of a personal and wholly insignificant grouse against life. It is just a piece of rhythmical grumbling."

This statement is prominently displayed by Mrs. Valerie Eliot in her excellent decipherment and elucidation of *The Waste Land* manuscript. If it is more than an expression of her husband's genuine modesty, it appears to imply that he considered his own poem, as he considered *Hamlet*, an inadequate projection of its author's tangled emotions, a Potemkin village rather than a proper objective correlative. Yet no one will wish away the entire civilizations and cities, wars, hordes of people, religions of East and West, and exhibits from many literatures in many languages that lined the Thames in Eliot's ode to dejection. And even if London was only his state of mind at the time, the picture he paints of it is convincing. His remark to Spencer, made after a lapse of years, perhaps catches up another regret, that the poem emphasized his *Groll* at the expense of much else in his nature. It identified him with a sustained severity of tone, with pulpited (though brief) citations of Biblical and Sophoclean anguish, so that he became an Ezekiel or at least a Tiresias. (In the original version John the Divine made a Christian third among the prophets.) While Eliot did not wish to be considered merely a satirist in his earlier verse, he did not welcome either the public assumption that his poetic mantle had become a hairshirt.

In its early version *The Waste Land* was woven out of more kinds of material, and was therefore less grave and less organized. The first two sections had an overall title (each had its own title as well), "He Do the Police in Different Voices," a quotation from *Our Mutual Friend.* Dickens has the widow Higden say to her adopted child, "Sloppy is a beautiful reader of a newspaper. He do the Police in different voices." Among the many voices in the first version, Eliot placed at the very beginning a long, conversational passage describing an evening on the town, starting at "Tom's place" (a rather arch use of his own name), moving on to a brothel, and concluding with a bathetic sunrise:

> First we had a couple of feelers down at Tom's place,
> There was old Tom, boiled to the eyes, blind . . .
> —("I turned up an hour later down at Myrtle's place.
> What d'y' mean, she says, at two o'clock in the morning,
> I'm not in business here for guys like you;
> We've only had a raid last week, I've been warned
> twice . . .
> So I got out to see the sunrise, and walked home.

This vapid prologue Eliot decided, apparently on his own, to expunge, and went straight into the now familiar beginning of the poem.

Other voices were expunged by Eliot's friend Ezra Pound, who called himself the "sage homme" (male mid-wife) of the poem. Pound had already published in 1920 his own elegy on a shipwrecked man, *Hugh Selwyn Mauberley.* Except in the title, the hero is unnamed, and like Eliot's protagonist, he is more an observing consciousness than a person, as he moves through salons, esthetic movements, dark thoughts of wartime deaths. But Mauberley's was an esthetic quest, and Eliot deliberately omitted this from his poem in favor of a spiritual one. (He would combine the two later in *Four Quartets*.) When Eliot was shown *Mauberley* in manuscript, he had remarked that the meaning of a section in Part II was not so clear as it might be, and Pound revised it accordingly.

Pound's criticism of *The Waste Land* was not of its meaning; he liked its despair and was indulgent of its neo-Christian hope. He dealt instead with its stylistic adequacy and freshness. For example, there was an extended, unsuccessful imitation of *The Rape of the Lock* at the beginning of "The Fire Sermon." It described the lady Fresca (imported to the waste land from "Gerontion" and one day to be exported to the States for the soft drink trade). Instead of making her toilet like Pope's Belinda, Fresca is going to it, like Joyce's Bloom. Pound warned Eliot that since Pope had done the couplets better, and Joyce the defecation, there was no point in another round. To this shrewd advice we are indebted for the disappearance of such lines as:

> The white-armed Fresca blinks, and yawns, and gapes,
> Aroused from dreams of love and pleasant rapes.
> Electric summons of the busy bell
> Brings brisk Amanda to destroy the spell . . .
> Leaving the bubbling beverage to cool,
> Fresca slips softly to the needful stool,
> Where the pathetic tale of Richardson
> Eases her labour till the deed is done . . .
> This ended, to the steaming bath she moves,
> Her tresses fanned by little flutt'ring Loves;
> Odours, confected by the cunning French,
> Disguise the good old hearty female stench.

The episode of the typist was originally much longer and more laborious:

> A bright kimono wraps her as she sprawls
> In nerveless torpor on the window seat;
> A touch of art is given by the false
> Japanese print, purchased in Oxford Street.

Pound found the décor difficult to believe: "Not in that lodging house?" The stanza was removed. When he read the later stanza,

> —Bestows one final patronising kiss,
> And gropes his way, finding the stairs unlit;
> And at the corner where the stable is,
> Delays only to urinate, and spit,

he warned that the last two lines were "probably over the mark," and Eliot acquiesced by cancelling them.

Pound persuaded Eliot also to omit a number of poems that were for a time intended to be placed between the poem's sections, then at the end of it. One was a renewed thrust at poor Bleistein, drowned now but still haplessly Jewish and luxurious under water:

> Full fathom five your Bleistein lies
> Under the flatfish and the squids.
>
> Graves' Disease in a dead jew's/man's eyes!
> Where the crabs have eat the lids . . .
>
> That is lace that was his nose . . .
>
> Roll him gently side to side,
> See the lips unfold unfold
>
> From the teeth, gold in gold. . . .

Pound urged that this, and several other mortuary poems, did not add anything, either to *The Waste Land* or to Eliot's previous work. He had already written "the longest poem in the English langwidge. Don't try to bust all records by prolonging it three pages further." As a result of this resmithying by *il miglior fabbro*, the poem gained immensely in concentration. Yet Eliot, feeling too solemnized by it, thought of prefixing some humorous doggerel by Pound about its composition. Later, in a more resolute effort to escape the limits set by *The Waste Land*, he wrote *Fragment of an Agon*, and eventually, "somewhere the other side of despair," turned to drama.

Eliot's remark to Spencer calls *The Waste Land* a personal poem. His critical theory was that the artist should seek impersonality, but this was probably intended not so much as a nostrum as an antidote, a means to direct emotion rather than let it spill. His letters indicate that he regarded his poems as consequent upon his experiences. When a woman in Dublin (Mrs. Josephine MacNeill, from whom I heard the account) remarked that Yeats had never really felt anything, Eliot asked in consternation, "How can you say that?" *The Waste Land* compiled many of the nightmarish feelings he had suffered during the seven years from 1914 to 1921, that is, from his coming to England until his temporary collapse.

Thanks to the letters quoted in Mrs. Valerie Eliot's introduction, and to various biographical leaks, the incidents of these years begin to take shape. In 1914 Eliot, then on a travelling fellowship from Harvard, went to study for the summer at Marburg. The outbreak of war obliged him to make his way, in a less leisurely fashion than he had intended, to Oxford. There he worked at his doctoral dissertation on F. H. Bradley's *Appearance and Reality*. The year 1914-1915 proved to be pivotal. He came to three interrelated decisions. The first was to give up the appearance of the philosopher for the reality of the poet, though he equivocated about this by continuing to write reviews for philosophical journals for some time thereafter. The second was to marry, and the third to remain in England. He was helped to all three decisions by Ezra Pound, whom he met in September 1914. Pound had come to England in 1908 and was convinced (though he changed his mind later) that this was the country most congenial to the literary life. He encouraged Eliot to marry and settle, and he read the poems that no one had been willing to publish and pronounced his verdict, that Eliot "has actually trained himself *and* modernized himself *on his own*." Harriet Monroe, the editor of *Poetry*, must publish them, beginning with "The Love Song of J. Alfred Prufrock." It took Pound some time to bring her to the same view, and it was not until June 1915 that Eliot's first publication took place. This was also the month of his first marriage, on June 26. His wife was Vivien Haigh-Wood, and Eliot remained, like Merlin with another Vivian, under her spell, beset and possessed by her intricacies for fifteen years and more.

What the newlyweds were like is recorded by Bertrand Russell, whom Eliot had known at Harvard. In a letter of July 1915, which he quotes in his *Autobiography*, Russell wrote of dining with them: "I expected her to be terrible, from his mysteriousness; but she was not so bad. She is light, a little vulgar, adventurous, full of life—an artist I think he said, but I should have thought her an actress. He is exquisite and listless; she says she married him to stimulate him, but finds she can't do it. Obviously he married in order to be stimulated. I think she will soon be tired of him. He is ashamed of his marriage, and very grateful if one is kind to her." Vivien was to dabble in painting, fiction, and verse, her mobile aspirations an aspect of her increasing instability.

Eliot's parents did not take well to their son's doings, though they did not, as has been said by Robert Sencourt, cut him off. His father, president of the Hydraulic Press Brick Company of St. Louis, had expected his son to remain a philosopher, and his mother, though a poet herself, did not like the *vers libre* of "Prufrock" any better than the free and easy marriage. To both parents it seemed that bright hopes were being put aside for a vague profession in the company of a vague woman in a country only too distinctly at war. They asked to see the young couple, but Vivien Eliot was frightened by the perils of the crossing, perhaps also by those of the arrival. So Eliot, already feeling "a broken Coriolanus," as Prufrock felt a Hamlet *manqué*, took the ship alone in August for the momentous interview.

His parents urged him to return with his wife to a university career in the States. He refused: he would be a poet, and England provided a better atmosphere in which to write. They urged him not to give up his dissertation when it was so near completion, and to this he consented. He parted on good enough terms to request their financial help when he got back to London, and they sent money to him handsomely, as he acknowledged—not handsomely enough, however, to release him from the necessity of very hard work. He taught for a term at the High Wycombe Grammar School, between Oxford and London, and then for two terms at Highgate Junior School. He completed his dissertation and was booked to sail on April 1, 1916, to take his oral examination at Harvard; when the crossing was cancelled, his academic gestures came to an end. In March 1917 he took the job with Lloyds Bank, in the Colonial and Foreign Department, at which he stuck for eight years.

During the early months of their marriage the Eliots were helped also by Russell, who gave them a room in his flat, an act of benevolence not without complications for all parties. Concerned for his wife's health, and fearful—it may be—that their sexual difficulties (perhaps involving psychic impotence on his part) might be a contributing factor, Eliot sent her off for a two-week holiday with Russell. The philosopher found the couple none the less devoted to each other, but noted in Mrs. Eliot a sporadic impulse to be cruel towards her husband, not with simple but with Dostoevskyan cruelty. "I am every day getting things more right between them," Russell boasted, "but I can't let them alone at present, and of course I myself get very much interested." The Dostoevskyan quality affected his imagery: "She is a person who lives on a knife-edge, and will end as a criminal or a saint—I don't know which yet. She has a perfect capacity for both."

The personal life out of which came Eliot's personal poem now began to be lived in earnest. Vivien Eliot suffered obscurely from nerves, her health was subject to frequent collapses, she complained of neuralgia, of insomnia. Her journal for January 1, 1919, records waking up with migraine, "the worst yet," and staying in bed all day without moving; on September 7, 1919, she records "bad pain in right side, very very nervous." Ezra Pound, who knew her well, was worried that the passage in *The Waste Land*,

> "My nerves are bad to-night. Yes, bad. Stay with me.
> "Speak to me. Why do you never speak? Speak.
> "What are you thinking of? What thinking? What?
> "I never know what you are thinking. Think."

59

might be too photographic. But Vivien Eliot, who offered her own comments on her husband's verse (and volunteered two excellent lines for the lowlife dialogue in "A Game of Chess")[1] marked the same passage as "Wonderful." She relished the presentation of her symptoms in broken metre. She was less keen, however, on another line from this section, "The ivory men make company between us," and got her husband to remove it. Presumably its implications were too close to the quick of their marital difficulties. The reference may have been to Russell, whose attentions to Vivien were intended to keep the two together. Years afterwards Eliot made a fair copy of *The Waste Land* in his own handwriting, and reinserted the line from memory. (It should now be added to the final text.) But he had implied his feelings six months after his marriage when he wrote in a letter to Conrad Aiken, "I have lived through material for a score of long poems in the last six months."

Russell commented less sympathetically about the Eliots later, "I was fond of them both, and endeavoured to help them in their troubles until I discovered that their troubles were what they enjoyed." Eliot was capable of estimating the situation shrewdly himself. In his poem, "The Death of Saint Narcissus," which *Poetry* was to publish in 1917 and then, probably because he withdrew it as too close to the knuckle, failed to do so, and which he thought for a time of including in *The Waste Land*, Eliot wrote of his introspective saint, "his flesh was in love with the burning arrows. . . . As he embraced them his white skin surrendered itself to the redness of blood, and satisfied him." For Eliot, however, the search for suffering was not contemptible. He was remorseful about his

[1] "If you don't like it you can get on with it
What you get married for if you don't want to have children"

own real or imagined feelings, he was self-sacrificing about hers, he thought that remorse and sacrifice, not to mention affection, had value. In the Grail legends which underlie *The Waste Land*, the Fisher King suffers a Dolorous Stroke that maims him sexually. In Eliot's case the Dolorous Stroke had been marriage. He was helped thereby to the poem's initial clash of images, "April is the cruellest month," as well as to hollow echoes of Spenser's *Prothalamion* ("Sweet Thames, run softly till I end my song"). From the barren winter of his academic labors Eliot had been roused to the barren springtime of his nerve-wracked marriage. His life spread into paradox.

Other events of these years seem reflected in the poem. The war, though scarcely mentioned, exerts pressure. In places the poem may be a covert memorial to Henry Ware Eliot, the unforgiving father of the ill-adventured son. Vivien Eliot's journal records on January 8, 1919, "Cable came saying Tom's father is dead. Had to wait all day till Tom came home and then to tell him. *Most terrible*." Eliot's first explicit statement of his intention to write a long poem comes in letters written later in this year. The references to "the king my father's death" probably derive as much from this actual death as from *The Tempest*, to which Eliot's notes evasively refer. As for the drowning of the young sailor, whether he is Ferdinand or a Phoenician, the war furnished Eliot with many examples, such as Jean Verdenal, a friend from his Sorbonne days, who was killed in the Dardanelles. (Verdenal has received the posthumous distinction of being called Eliot's lover, but in fact the rumors of homosexuality—not voiced directly in Sencourt's biography but whispered in all its corners—remain unwitnessed.) But the drowning may be as well an extrapolation of Eliot's feeling that he was now fatherless as well as rudderless. The fact that the principal speaker appears in a new guise in the last section, with its imagery of possible resurrection, suggests that the drowning is to be taken symbolically rather than literally, as the end of youth. Eliot was addicted to the portrayal of characters who had missed their chances, become old before they had really been young. So the drowned sailor, like the buried corpse, may be construed as the young Eliot, himself an experienced sailor, shipwrecked in or about *l'an trentièsme de son eage*, like the young Pound in the first part of *Hugh Selwyn Mauberley* or Mauberley himself later in that poem, memorialized only by an oar.

It has been thought that Eliot wrote *The Waste Land* in Switzerland while recovering from a breakdown. But much of it was written earlier, some in 1914 and some, if Conrad Aiken is to be believed, even before. A letter to John Quinn indicates that much of it was on paper in May 1921. The breakdown, or rather, the rest cure, did give Eliot enough time to fit the pieces together and add what was necessary. At the beginning of October 1921 he consulted a prominent neurologist, who advised three months away from remembering "the profit and loss" in Lloyds Bank. When the bank had agreed, Eliot went first to Margate and stayed for a month from October 11. There he reported with relief to Richard Aldington that his "nerves" came not from overwork but from an "aboulie" (Hamlet's and Prufrock's disease) "and emotional derangement which has been a lifelong affliction." But, whatever reassurance this diagnosis afforded, he resolved to consult Dr. Roger Vittoz, a psychiatrist in Lausanne. He rejoined Vivien and on November 18 went with her to Paris. It seems fairly certain that he discussed the poem at that time with Ezra Pound. In Lausanne, where he went by himself, Eliot worked on it and sent revisions to

Pound and to Vivien. Some of the letters exchanged between him and Pound survive. By early January 1922 he was back in London, making final corrections. The poem was published in October.

The manuscript had its own history. In gratitude to John Quinn, the New York lawyer and patron of the arts, Eliot presented it to him. Quinn died in 1924, and most of his possessions were sold at auction; some, however, including the manuscript, were inherited by his sister. When the sister died, her daughter put many of Quinn's papers in storage. But in the early 1950's she searched among them and found the manuscript, which she then sold to the Berg Collection of the New York Public Library. The then curator enjoyed exercising seignorial rights over the collection, and kept secret the whereabouts of the manuscript. After his death its existence was divulged, and Valerie Eliot was persuaded to do her knowledgeable edition.

She did so the more readily, perhaps, because her husband had always hoped that the manuscript would turn up as evidence of Pound's critical genius. It is a classic document. No one will deny that it is weaker throughout than the final version. Pound comes off very well indeed; his importance is comparable to that of Louis Bouilhet in the history of composition of *Madame Bovary*. Yeats, who also sought and received Pound's help, described it to Lady Gregory: "To talk over a poem with him is like getting you to put a sentence into dialect. All becomes clear and natural." Pound could not be intimidated by pomposity, even Baudelairean pomposity:

> London, the swarming life you kill and breed,
> Huddled between the concrete and the sky;
> Responsive to the momentary need,
> Vibrates unconscious to its formal destiny.

63

Next to this he wrote "B-ll-S." (His comments appear in red ink on the printed transcription that is furnished along with photographs of the manuscript.) Pound was equally peremptory about a passage that Eliot seems to have cherished, perhaps because of childhood experiences in sailing. It was the depiction at the beginning of "Death by Water" of a long voyage, a modernizing and americanizing of Ulysses' final voyage as given by Dante, but joined with sailing experiences of Eliot's youth:

> Kingfisher weather, with a light fair breeze,
> Full canvas, and the eight sails drawing well.
> We beat around the cape and laid our course
> From the Dry Salvages to the eastern banks.
> A porpoise snored upon the phosphorescent swell,
> A triton rang the final warning bell
> Astern, and the sea rolled, asleep.

From these lines Pound was willing to spare only

> with a light fair breeze
> We beat around the cape from the Dry Salvages.
> A porpoise snored on the swell.

All the rest was—seamanship and literature. It became clear that the whole passage might as well go, and Eliot asked humbly if he should delete Phlebas as well. But Pound was as eager to preserve the good as to expunge the bad: he insisted that Phlebas stay because of the earlier references to the drowned Phoenician sailor. With equal taste, he made almost no change in the last section of the poem, which Eliot always considered to be the best, perhaps because it led into his subsequent verse. It marked the resumption of almost continuous form.

Eliot did not bow to all his friend's revisions. Pound

feared the references to London might sound like Blake, and objected specifically to the lines,

> To where Saint Mary Woolnoth kept the time,
> With a dead sound on the final stroke of nine.

Eliot wisely retained them, only changing "time" to "hours." Next to the passage,

> "You gave me hyacinths first a year ago;
> "They called me the hyacinth girl,"

Pound marked "Marianne," and evidently feared—though Mrs. Eliot's note indicates that he has now forgotten and denies it—that the use of quotation marks would look like an imitation of Marianne Moore. (He had warned Miss Moore of the equivalent danger of sounding like Eliot in a letter of December 16, 1918.) But Eliot, for whom the moment in the Hyacinth garden had obsessional force—it was based on feelings, though not on a specific incident in his own life—made no change.

Essentially Pound could do for Eliot what Eliot could not do for himself. There was some reciprocity, not only in *Mauberley* but in the *Cantos*. When the first three of these appeared in *Poetry* in 1917, Eliot offered criticism which was followed by their being completely altered. It appears, from the revised versions, that he objected to the elaborate windup, and urged a more direct confrontation of the reader and the material. A similar theory is at work in Pound's changes in *The Waste Land*. Chiefly by excision, he enabled Eliot to tighten his form and get "an outline," as he wrote in a complimentary letter of January 24, 1922. The same letter berated himself for "always exuding my deformative secretions in my own stuff . . ."

65

and for "going into nacre and objets d'art." Yet if this was necessity for Pound, he soon resolved to make a virtue of it, and perhaps partially in reaction in Eliot's form, he studied out means of loosening his own in the *Cantos*. The fragments which Eliot wished to shore and reconstitute Pound was willing to keep unchanged, and instead of mending consciousness, he allowed it to remain "disjunct" and its experiences to remain "intermittent." Fits and starts, "spots and dots," seemed to Pound to render reality much more closely than the outline to which he had helped his friend. He was later to feel that he had gone wrong, and made a botch instead of a work of art. Notwithstanding his doubts, the *Cantos*, with their violent upheaval of sequence and location, stand as a rival eminence to *The Waste Land* in modern verse.

Helen Gardner *THE WASTE LAND*: PARIS 1922

FIFTY YEARS ago last October
The Waste Land appeared in
the first number of *The Criterion*, and later in the same
month Eliot packed up and posted to John Quinn, the
wealthy New York banker, as token of his gratitude for
Quinn's generous patronage and help, a parcel. It con-
tained what Eliot described as "the MSS of the Waste
Land . . . when I say MSS, I mean that it is partly MSS
and partly typescript, with Ezra's and my alterations
scrawled all over it."[1] This famous collection of docu-
ments was thought to have been lost, since it was not in
the Quinn sale, nor was it referred to in his will. In fact
it passed to his sister and from her to her daughter,
Quinn's niece, to end up in 1958 in the Berg Collection
in the New York Public Library. The curator, for reasons
that remain obscure, did not announce its presence there
until 1968. It was finely edited in facsimile with tran-
scripts, notes, and introduction by Mrs. Valerie Eliot in

[1] Quotations from Eliot's letters for which no reference is given
are taken from Mrs. Eliot's introduction to *The Waste Land: a
Facsimile and Transcript* (1971).

67

time for the jubilee of the poem. Everything I have to say is dependent on Mrs. Eliot's work. Her skill in deciphering and identifying hands, her admirably succinct and informative introduction, and her notes, as remarkable for the research they embody as for their splendid economy, make this edition a distinguished feat of scholarship.

We speak, for convenience, of the "manuscript of *The Waste Land*." But we should be careful not to speak of "the first version," as if what we have here is a kind of "*Ur-Waste Land*." Nor should we speak of "the original version." There is only one version of *The Waste Land*, and that is the published text. We are not faced here with anything like the two versions of *The Rape of the Lock* or *The Dunciad*, or the two versions that exist of many of Yeats's early poems, or of the poems of Wordsworth and Auden. In all these cases poems their authors thought of as finished, and had presented to the world as finished, they later decided to alter and revise. The material Eliot sent to Quinn was not a first or original version in any sense. It was working material of very varied kinds: manuscript first drafts, fragments of manuscript drafts, manuscript fair copies, typed drafts, typed copies, carbons; and he included with drafts of the poem drafts of other unpublished poems and unfinished fragments on which he had drawn for lines and passages, three of which he had worked up into fair copies, thinking to publish them as a kind of appendix to *The Waste Land*.

The chronology of the writing of *The Waste Land* is obscure, even with the help of Mrs. Eliot's introduction. It seems likely that it will always remain so. Pound is dead, and it is all fifty years ago. Eliot's own summary statement was made in a tribute to Pound in 1946 where he wrote, "It was in 1922 that I placed before him in Paris the manuscript of a sprawling chaotic poem called

68

The Waste Land which left his hands reduced to about half its size, in the form in which it appears in print."[2] Eliot was not here concerned to give a detailed account of the writing of *The Waste Land*; but to pay tribute to Pound. And when, in June 1922, Eliot wrote to Quinn "I have written, mostly when I was at Lausanne for treatment last winter, a long poem of about 450 words [he meant, of course, *lines*]," he was again not concerned to give an accurate account of the poem's gestation but to discuss its publication.

The first we hear of *The Waste Land* is at the end of 1919. Eliot, who had referred in a letter to Quinn of 5 November to "a poem I have in mind," wrote to his mother in December that his New Year resolution for 1920 was "to write a long poem I have had on my mind for a long time." But through almost all of 1920 he was occupied with preparing *The Sacred Wood* for the press and with checking its proofs. It appeared in November 1920. By May of 1921 he was able to inform Quinn that "a long poem" that he was "wishful to finish" was now "partly on paper." The words "wishful to finish," as well as "partly on paper" suggest that a substantial portion of the poem was extant by May 1921 either in holograph or typed. By September, however, after a gruelling summer, his health was so bad that his wife arranged for him to see a specialist who declared that he must go away for three months alone. His friend Conrad Aiken, who was living in London in the autumn of 1921, tells us that Eliot told him "although every evening he went home to his flat hoping that he could start writing again, and with every confidence that the material was *there* and waiting, night after night, the hope proved illusory: the sharpened

[2] "Ezra Pound," *Poetry Chicago* (September 1946), reprinted *New English Weekly* (31 October, 7 November 1946).

pencil lay unused by the untouched sheet of paper."[3] Lloyds gave him three months' sick leave, and he went in mid-October to Margate, and then in November, via Paris, where he left his wife, to a clinic in Lausanne for treatment. Pound had been settled in Paris since June and no doubt Eliot saw him on his way through. It is possible that Eliot showed him the chaotic poem he had been working on at Margate; but Mrs. Eliot tells me that she thinks it unlikely that he lingered in Paris on his way to Lausanne, as he was anxious to begin treatment as soon as possible. After all, he had only three months' leave and one month of it had already been spent at Margate. In early January 1922 Eliot returned to London via Paris, and on this occasion he stopped for some days with Pound. On 21 February Pound wrote to Quinn: "Eliot came back from his Lausanne specialist looking OK; and with a damn good poem (19 pages) in his suitcase; same finished up here."

The description of the poem as being "19 pages" echoes the famous letter of Pound to Eliot dated by Pound "Paris, 24 Saturnus, An I," interpreted by Paige as 24 December 1921. Until I had the privilege of a preview of Professor Kenner's article, I had ignorantly accepted Paige's date and found it very puzzling. I now gratefully acknowledge that his authoritative correction of the date to 24 January 1922 clears up some, though not all, of my difficulties. As he rightly observes, by no feat of juggling can one arrive at 19 pages from the typed drafts. Eliot must have retyped the poem, in accordance with decisions that he and Pound had reached in Paris, when he returned to London and posted this retyping, or a

[3] "An Anatomy of Melancholy," in *T. S. Eliot the Man and His Work*, edited Allen Tate, *Sewanee Review* (January to March 1966), and Chatto and Windus (London, 1967), p. 195.

70

carbon of it, to Pound in Paris for further comment. If this is so, it makes Pound's statement to Quinn that Eliot came back from Lausanne with "a damn good poem (19 pages)" hardly accurate. But what are we to make of Pound's final words: "Same finished up here"? They seem hardly an adequate description of the drastic cutting and rewriting presented by the drafts. The accepted legend of Pound and Eliot sitting down together in one long marathon session in Paris in January 1922 to carve *The Waste Land* out of chaos hardly tallies with Pound's description of what happened there as a "finishing up."

In his letter of "24 Saturnus, An I," enthusiastically acknowledging the revised poem as "MUCH improved," Pound advised that the "remaining superfluities," that is, the shorter poems Eliot had thought of printing with *The Waste Land*, should be abolished; or, if Eliot felt that he must keep them, they should be at the beginning of the volume. For, he declared, "The thing now runs from 'April . . .' to 'shantih' without a break. That is 19 pages, and let us say the longest poem in the English langwidge. Don't try to bust all records by prolonging it three pages further."[4] He concluded with his little self-congratulatory squib on himself as Eliot's man-midwife, the poem headed

SAGE HOMME

These are the poems of Eliot
By the Uranian Muse begot;
A Man their Mother was,
A Muse their Sire.

How did the printed Infancies result
From Nuptials thus doubly difficult?

[4] *Letters of Ezra Pound*, edited D. D. Paige (1941), pp. 233-34.

If you must needs enquire
Know diligent Reader
That on each occasion
Ezra performed the caesarian Operation.

What Pound and Eliot did in their January meeting in Paris when the poem was "finished up," and in correspondence when the revised manuscript seems to have shuffled to and fro between London and Paris may have been only the culmination of a longer process of criticism and discussion than is usually supposed. I suspect that it was a long and difficult pregnancy and birth that Pound assisted at.

I have not seen the original documents, and they have not been subjected to intensive examination. One would like to know what kinds of paper were used and what, if discoverable, were their origins. No doubt the kind of experts who testified in the Hiss case could tell us not only about the different typewriters used but also whether all the typed drafts were typed by the same person. But from the study of the facsimile I should like to make some tentative suggestions. It seems likely to me that when Eliot went to the Albemarle Hotel at Margate in October 1921 he took with him the typed drafts of Parts I and II and the greater part of Part III, which breaks off a few lines after the episode of the typist. (Professor Kenner points out that these were typed on two different typewriters: the unfinished Part III on typewriter A and Parts I and II on typewriter B.) I presume he also had with him a bundle of drafts and fragments of unworked-up poems, mostly in manuscript, but three of them typed, the longest, "The Death of the Duchess," being typed on typewriter B. There exists no typescript of the close of "The Fire Sermon"—the song of the daughters of the Thames, and their speeches—and for Parts IV and V we have Eliot's manuscripts, and typed copies of them made on a third machine and typed with a violet ribbon that Mrs. Eliot tells us was used by Pound. Whether Pound himself typed them, or Eliot did so on Pound's typewriter, it is impossible to guess. But it looks as if when Eliot wrote the close of "The Fire Sermon" and Parts IV and V he had not access to a typewriter. The long cancelled section (83 lines) that preceded the lyric on Phlebas the Phoenician is, with the lyric, very carefully and beautifully written out by Eliot in what is plainly a neat fair copy. He would hardly have taken all this trouble to write so neatly and clearly if he had had a typewriter available. The last section, "What the Thunder Said," on the other hand, is an untitled first draft, remarkably free until the close of any alteration or revision. This section we know was written at Lausanne, for Eliot said he was describing his own experience in writing it when he wrote in his essay on Pascal that some forms of illness were extremely favourable to literary composition, and added: "A piece of writing meditated, apparently without progress, for months or years, may suddenly take shape and word; and in this state long passages may be produced which require little or no retouch."[5] The draft strikingly exemplifies poetry that in this way "just came."

The question that teases me is when did Pound make the criticisms, comments, excisions, and queries that abound in the typescripts of the first three parts. Eliot could have posted his poem as far as it had gone from Margate and picked it up in Paris on his way to Lausanne. Or he could have left it with Pound in Paris on his way to Lausanne and Pound could have posted it to him there with comments and markings. But I wonder. Throughout

[5] *Essays Ancient and Modern* (1936), p. 142.

1920 and 1921 Pound was deeply concerned with Eliot's unhappy, even desperate, situation, and he was to and fro between London and the Continent. I cannot believe that if, as Eliot wrote to Quinn in May 1921, his "long poem" was by then "partly on paper" he had not shown what was there to Pound and discussed it with him. Pound's markings and comments may not all have been made at the same time. On some portions he has used both ink and pencil, and the marks themselves are of different kinds. Some are explanatory, making clear what the reader's objection is, as if they were to be communicated by post. Others are marks which suggest that a word or passage needs to be thought over or discussed: queries, boxing in of a word, or a squiggle against a line or word. These are the kind of marks one makes on a piece of work one is going to hand back to the author in person. The long unpublished poem "The Death of the Duchess," which Eliot quarried in for "A Game of Chess," is heavily annotated by Pound in the same kind of way as the typed drafts of *The Waste Land* are. Pound must have worked on this typescript before Eliot decided to use part of this poem for Part II, "A Game of Chess," and not go on with it. But "A Game of Chess" was read and commented on by Vivien Eliot and so must have been typed before Eliot went to Lausanne. I cannot help believing that when Eliot at last had a respite and time to give his mind to his long meditated long poem at Margate, some at least of Pound's criticisms were already there to be digested and absorbed for the rewriting of what had been written and for the completion of the whole at Lausanne. It seems possible that some of Pound's criticisms were made before the period of block that Aiken refers to, when Eliot found himself unable to go on with his poem.

It is impossible to overestimate Eliot's debt to Pound,

but it needs defining. Without Pound *The Waste Land* would have been very different from what it is; but we should not therefore assume that it would necessarily have been like the drafts, and that Eliot himself would not have drastically revised it before publication, as he revised his later poems. If my theory of the composition of *The Waste Land* is true, *The Waste Land*, the culmination of Eliot's early period, has a history not unlike that of *Little Gidding*, the culmination of his later period. He sent a first draft of this to John Hayward in July 1941 with a discouraged letter. Hayward wrote back agreeing that the poem was not the equal of its predecessors, but rightly pointing out that it presented a more difficult problem as it was to be a sum of the others, and urging Eliot to go on with it. But Eliot laid it aside apparently for a year, and when he came back to it to revise it he not only made a great many changes in wording but completely discarded the original ending of the interview with the "dead master" after the air-raid, and wrote an entirely different speech, although the first version was very beautiful. He also remade Part IV, which he knew was wrong, but which he could not see what to do with.[6] We should not assume that without Pound Eliot would have published some of the weaker passages in the drafts. But, as soon as one says this, one must add that it is highly doubtful whether, without Pound, *The Waste Land* would have been completed and published at all. The most important thing Pound gave Eliot was the support of a constant affection, encouragement, and belief. And he gave it at a time of deep discouragement verging on despair. It seems almost a miracle when one considers the circumstances

---

[6] I am at present working on the drafts of *Four Quartets* and the relevant sections of the Eliot-Hayward correspondence and refer to them with Mrs. Eliot's permission.

75

in which the poem was written that it was written at all.
To Eliot, struggling in ill health and overwork to com-
bine two obligations—his sense of his vocation as a poet,
and his duty to the unhappy girl he had married, who was
dependent on him—Pound's unwavering belief in his
friend's genius was the stimulus without which he might
not have found the courage to persevere. But in addition
to his selfless promotion of Eliot's interests as man and
poet, Pound showed, for all his bluster and boisterous-
ness, his slashings and damnings, an extreme selflessness
and sensitivity in the kind of criticism he gave. He con-
centrated on making the poem as good as Eliot could
make it. He gave his whole mind to the problem of "Was
this good verse?" "Is this the right word?" "Does this
strike a false note?" "Is this becoming monotonous?" He
makes no comment on the subject matter of the poem, its
religious or philosophic views, its lack of those "life-
enhancing" qualities whose absence later critics have de-
plored. It was Eliot's poem he was working on.[7] He shows
his genius as a critic in the applause he gives—"Echt,"
"OK"—to the most characteristically Eliotian lines and
passages. One's heart rises as one sees his "Stet" or "OK."
Vivien Eliot, like some of those to whom Eliot showed
his later poems, suggested words. She even supplied two
lines, and good ones. But Pound, with the exception of
the word "demotic," which he supplied on a carbon of
"The Fire Sermon," and the word "demobbed"—here
Mrs. Eliot tells me she is not absolutely certain it was his

[7] The publication of the drafts fully confirms Eliot's tribute to
Pound as a critic: "He was a marvellous critic because he didn't
try to turn you into an imitation of himself. He tried to see what
you were trying to do." (*Paris Review Interviews*, reprinted in
Writers at Work, introduced by Van Wyck Brooks, 2nd series,
1963, pp. 79-84.)

suggestion and he has not pencilled over a suggestion of Vivien Eliot's[8]—was content with scoring through or boxing in, or querying words and phrases he thought struck a false note, without proposing improvements. He expressed disquiet, or disapproval, and left it to Eliot to solve his own problems. His little *jeu d'esprit* just quoted was perfectly accurate. He was the midwife: the child that emerged into life was Eliot's. And Eliot found the right words in Dante when he saluted Pound as *il miglior fabbro*, the better craftsman.

Eliot said that when he used this phrase he did not mean to imply that Pound was only a craftsman; but he wanted in dedicating his poem to him to "honour the technical mastery and critical ability manifest in his own work, which had also done so much to turn *The Waste Land* from a jumble of good and bad passages into a poem."[9] This is a very good description of Pound's major surgery. Before the drafts turned up there was a general belief that Pound was responsible for the form of the poem, and that "all the transitions—or lack of them" in the poem "were due to the editor."[10] This is clearly not so. The famous inconsequence or discontinuity was there from the beginning and Pound's reduction did not turn an ordered sequence of action or thought into a cryptic puzzle. It was not linking passages that he removed. There never were any links in the poem as Eliot con-

[8] Mrs. Eliot tells me she thinks the writing is Vivien's, but that Pound believes that he supplied the word.

[9] "On a Recent Piece of Criticism," *Purpose* X, 2 (April to June 1938).

[10] See, for instance, Charles Norman, *Ezra Pound* (revised edition, 1969), p. 251. Eliot himself had made the position clear in his *Paris Review* interview in 1959, when, in response to the query, "Did the excisions change the intellectual structure of the poem?" he replied: "No, I think it was just as structureless, only in a more futile way, in the longer poem."

ceived it. At times, Pound, in his passion for concision, for packing meaning and omitting connectives that have syntactical or explanatory but not connotative functions, has left some phrases or lines obscure; but the major difficulty, the major originality, of *The Waste Land* was inherent in it from the beginning. It was, as originally drafted, to be a poem in violently contrasting styles which were to be juxtaposed, a poem of episodes following each other without narrative consequence, of allusions and quotations that drift across the mind. Its unity was to derive from its underlying theme of sterility, disordered desire, and impotent longing. Lines from unpublished poems and from fragments of poems jotted down and never worked up, some written many years before, came together in Eliot's mind, with memories of incidents, some perhaps long buried, some recent, and with reminiscences and echoes from older poets. It was enough that they were all related to a central core of profound feeling, a feeling summed in the title *The Waste Land*. It is uncertain when the poem acquired this title—possibly very late. But the title is its sum.

Eliot himself was responsible for the first big cut. Parts I and II in the typescript drafts have a general title that links them. They are headed "He Do the Police in Different Voices, Part I and Part II." I suppose this is another and unpoetical way of saying "I Tiresias have foresuffered all." The poem was to be an exercise in ventriloquism. The poet, like Sloppy reading to Betty Higden in *Our Mutual Friend*, is behind all the voices of men and women we are to be asked to listen to. The first part began with a passage of fifty-four lines in loose blank verse, describing a male night-out in Boston. This would seem a bold but unsuccessful experiment, inspired by *Ulysses*, to see whether the kind of material Joyce was engaged in

incorporating into the novel could be made available also
for poetry. It is a mild version of a visit to Night-town.
Ulysses had been appearing in the *Little Review* and had
made an immense impression on Eliot, and in some ways
in *The Waste Land* he was attempting to do for poetry
what Joyce had done for the novel. This description of
the night-out in Boston is the prelude to the first part as
we know it. We pass without transition from this vulgar
male voice to the lamenting, meditative voice of "April
is the cruellest month." Part II, then, reversed this pat-
tern, beginning with the elaborate poetical passage which
is the setting for the Lady of Situations and ending with
the vulgar female voice of poor Lil's false friend in the
pub. Eliot himself drew a pencil line through the Boston
passage. As there are no comments by Pound on it, Eliot
had presumably decided to drop it before he showed any
of his poem to Pound. It leaves the passage about Lil and
Albert as the one example of the low colloquial in the
poem, the more effective for its uniqueness. From here on
Eliot seems to have abandoned a rather over-schematic
plan. The excision of the Boston opening also makes the
poem open not with a mere episode but with the an-
nouncement of its true subject: "memory and desire."

Two other major cuts we owe to Pound. For his third
section, headed "The Fire Sermon," as in the second sec-
tion, "A Game of Chess," and the original draft of the
fourth section, Eliot began with literary parody, opening
it with some seventy lines in couplets devoted to Fresca,
a fashionable lady with aesthetic and literary pretensions.
On the carbon copy of this Pound has scrawled his
objections: "Too loose"—"rhyme drags it out to diffuse-
ness"—"trick of Pope etc not to let couple[t] diffuse
'em." On the top copy he has marked only an occasional
word with brackets, or by boxing it in, before crossing

out, with slashing strokes, as if he quickly saw the passage was beyond help. Eliot said, rather ruefully, in 1928 that Pound had induced him to destroy "what I thought an excellent set of couplets," "for," said he, "Pope has done this so well that you cannot do it better; and if you mean this as a burlesque, you had better suppress it, for you cannot parody Pope unless you can write better verse than Pope—and you can't."[11] Eliot accepted Pound's deletion of the whole passage and substituted the present evocative opening of the third part "The river's tent is broken!" It is written in pencil on the verso of the first leaf of the typescript. It breaks off with "By the waters," leaving us uncertain whether this passage was written at Margate and completed at Lausanne by the extension of the line to "By the waters of Leman I sat down and wept" or wholly at Lausanne. This revives the tone of the opening lines of the poem after our excursion into the world of Lil and Albert. It shows Eliot beginning to draw the poem together and moving away from its original ventriloquial base.

Pound's second major cut was his reduction of Part IV to the brief lyric on Phlebas the Phoenician. Eliot had written out "Part IV" in a beautiful, neat, fair copy, with the title "Death by Water," dividing it by asterisks into three sections. The first section consisted of three quatrains on the sailor:

> The sailor, attentive to the chart or to the sheets,
> A concentrated will against the tempest and the tide,
> Retains, even ashore, in public bars or streets
> Something inhuman, clean and dignified.
>
> Even the drunken ruffian who descends
> Illicit backstreet stairs, to reappear,

[11] Introduction to *Selected Poems* of Ezra Pound (1928).

For the derision of his sober friends,
Staggering, or limping with a comic gonorrhea,

From his trade with wind and sea and snow, as they
Are, he is, with 'much seen and much endured',
Foolish, impersonal, innocent or gay,
Liking to be shaved, combed, scented, manucured.

Against these quatrains Pound has written "Bad—but
cant attack until I get typescript." The second section is
a first-person narrative (seventy-one lines) in blank verse,
parodying Tennysonian narrative blank verse, telling of
a voyage, setting its course from the Dry Salvages, and
sailing to the eastern banks to fish cod. It ends with ship-
wreck. The third section is the Phlebas lyric. On the type-
script, typed with his violet ribbon, Pound has made an
initial attempt to break up the quatrains and the regular-
ity of the blank verse before deciding, as with the cou-
plets on Fresca, that the passage was beyond salvage. He
crossed through, leaving only Phlebas intact. When Eliot
was back in London he wrote to Pound with various
queries and among them: "Perhaps better omit Phlebas
too??" To which Pound replied: "I DO advise keeping
Phlebas. In fact I more'n advise. Phlebas is an integral
part of the poem; the card pack introduces him, the
drowned phoen. sailor. And he is needed ABsolootly
where he is. Must stay in."[12] The lines on Phlebas are a
free translation of the close of the French poem "Dans
le Restaurant" which Eliot had published in his 1920
volume. Reappearing in Madame Sosostris's wicked pack
of cards, the Phoenician sailor is gathered up, like so
much of Eliot's early poetry and life, into *The Waste
Land*, and as Pound rightly saw is needed absolutely
where he is. Eliot's intense feeling for the sea, and for

[12] *Letters of Ezra Pound*, p. 237.

sailing and sailors, expressed in the long cancelled passage, found later and more adequate expression at the close of *Ash Wednesday*, in *Marina*, and finally in *The Dry Salvages*. In *The Waste Land* it gave him a beautiful passage, one of the few happy memories in the poem, at the close:

> The boat responded
> Gaily, to the hand expert with sail and oar
> The sea was calm, your heart would have responded
> Gaily, when invited, beating obedient
> To controlling hands.

One shorter passage that Pound struck out, writing a rude word against it in the typescript, was an address to London that gave Eliot much trouble. It stands in the typescript between the episode with Mr. Eugenides and the episode of the typist. On a separate sheet there is a pencil draft of two apostrophes to London. At the top is the passage beginning "O City, City, I have heard and hear/The pleasant whining of a mandoline." Then after a line drawn across the paper comes a much-worked-over draft of this second apostrophe. Presumably Eliot composed the two passages at much the same time—they contrast in mood—and put them on one side to await a place for them in the poem. I rather regret that Eliot accepted Pound's advice here and did not instead struggle to improve a potentially impressive vision of London as a city of automata, its people "bound upon the wheel," "Phantasmal gnomes," only alive in "the awareness of the observing eye," which sees them as "pavement toys." It picks up the vision of the crowd flowing over London Bridge at the close of the first part, and makes a break between the two episodes of Mr. Eugenides and the typist, as the "O City, City" passage was to do between the close of the typist episode and the song of the daughters of the Thames.

These were Pound's major cuts. They accord with Eliot's tribute to him for turning "a jumble of good and bad passages into a poem." But in addition to the removing of the couplets on Fresca, with their feeble social satire, the slackly written narrative of the shipwreck, and the over-rhetorical apostrophe to London, Pound worked hard revising, and in one case severely reducing, two passages. The most striking is the famous episode of the typist, a passage that greatly impressed the poem's first readers but that seems less impressive today. This episode originally consisted of seventeen regular quatrains (sixty-eight lines) and was reduced by Eliot, largely in accordance with Pound's criticism, to some forty lines. Pound worked on both a typescript and a carbon, the carbon apparently first, since the typescript has a note "vide other copy." His general comment was "Verse not interesting enough as verse to warrant so much of it." His revision had two ends in view. He worked to destroy the regularity of the quatrains, which after the revision only establish themselves at the climax of the passage, the rhymes at the beginning being irregular, and he worked to reduce what seemed to him irrelevant and sometimes contradictory social detail. Eliot, while accepting the general line of Pound's criticism, did not accept it in all its details. Pound, showing an unexpected modesty, struck out the typist's "stays," which Eliot retained: though he accepted Pound's comment "probably over the mark" and deleted the young man's original exit lines:

> And at the corner where the stable is,
> Delays only to urinate, and spit.

He preserved, in spite of Pound's striking it out, the description of the young man which has set some sensitive critics' teeth on edge:

> One of the low on whom assurance sits
> As a silk hat on a Bradford millionaire.

But Pound's power to recognize the excellent appears again when he comes to the last six stanzas. Apart from the two lines that dismiss the young man, he leaves them, with an "Echt" against the Tiresias quatrain, and only an explosion at the use of "may" in the line "Across her brain one half-formed thought may pass": "Make up yr mind you Tiresias if you know know damn well or else you dont." He had made a similar comment earlier "Perhaps be damned."

The other passage Pound worked hard on is the opening of "A Game of Chess." Here again he disliked the regularity of the metre: "Too tum-pum at a stretch" he wrote against the first three lines, and later on "too penty," presumably meaning too much pentameter. The latter is his comment on the line "Filled all the desert with inviolable voice," where he boxed in the word "inviolable." Luckily Eliot ignored this and did not destroy this beautiful line. Pound was concerned to break up the even movement of the pentameters and in doing so to tighten, condense, and concentrate, by removing connectives and explanatory phrases and clauses. Thus he took out the words "Upon the hearth" in the lines

> Upon the hearth huge sea-wood fed with copper
> Burned green and orange, framed by the coloured stone.

They are unnecessary. One can see the weakness of

> Above the antique mantel was displayed
> In pigment, but so lively, you had thought

84

> A window gave upon the sylvan scene,
> The change of Philomel. . . .

Pound scored through "but so lively, you had thought" with the comment "had is the weakest point." Eliot retrenched three lines to two, making his second an alexandrine, thus simultaneously condensing and making the rhythm more flexible:

> Above the antique mantel was displayed
> As though a window gave upon the sylvan scene
> The change of Philomel . . . .

Similarly the original lines

> And still she cried (and still the world pursues)
> Jug-Jug, into the dirty ear of [death] lust;

are less impressive than " 'Jug-Jug' to dirty ears."

At times in his passion for loading every rift with ore Pound left lines that are rather cryptic. I was puzzled for years over what was meant by

> And other withered stumps of time
> Were told upon the walls,

though one can see why Pound objected to the lines in the draft:

> And other tales, from the old stumps and bloody ends
>   of time
> Were told upon the walls.

In some of Pound's criticisms and deletions one is aware of a certain lack of response to some strains in Eliot's poetry. His objection to "inviolable" shows a resistance seen elsewhere to the romantic and tender strain in the poem. Thus he also scored out "forgetful" in the lines

Winter kept us warm, covering
Earth in forgetful snow.

This may have been an objection to a transferred epithet;
but he also placed his squiggles and a query against

'You gave me hyacinths first a year ago;
They called me the hyacinth girl.'

He put against this the cryptic word "Marianne." He de-
leted the bracketed quotation that follows Madame Sosos-
tris's production of the card of the drowned Phoenician
sailor: "(Those are pearls that were his eyes. Look!)."
On these occasions Eliot resisted; but he acquiesced in
Pound's removal of another quotation that also com-
ments on Madame Sosostris's visions:

I see crowds of people walking round in a ring.
(I John saw these things and heard them).

He also boxed in the word "little" in a line Eliot dropped;
an unspoken response of the silent man to the woman's
insistent questions in "A Game of Chess":

'What is that noise now? What is the wind doing?'
                                        Carrying
Away the little light dead people.

Presumably Pound felt "little" to be a trifle sentimental.
The lines are, as Mrs. Eliot says, a reminiscence of
Dante's Paolo and Francesca who "go together and seem
so light upon the wind." I regret their loss.

Pound seems to have had rather a down on city
churches: he scored through

To where Saint Mary Woolnoth kept the time
With a dead sound on the final stroke of nine,

which Eliot mercifully kept and also the three lines with which the typescript of "The Fire Sermon" breaks off:

Fading at last, behind the flying feet,
There where the tower was traced against the night
Of Michael Paternoster Royal, red and white.

Eliot gave up St. Michael Paternoster Royal, but gave us St. Magnus Martyr instead in a passage that we have only in draft on which Pound has not worked. Again where Pound rightly objected to Madame Sosostris saying "I look in vain," which is an impossible locution for her, it is odd that he also objected to "there you feel free" in the line "In the mountains, there you feel free," where the cliché has great pathos. Here again Eliot resisted the cut.

It is natural to concentrate first on Pound's work on the drafts. There is, I think, no other example in literature of a poet submitting his work for criticism to another poet of equal stature and accepting radical criticism. It was Eliot's habit to submit his work to the criticism of his friends, or, with his plays, to the criticism of producers and actors. He was able to accept Pound's surgery gratefully because they shared a common belief in poetry as an art demanding severe discipline and in the poem as a thing made with care and skill. So, later on, if a friend queried a word or line, he accepted with seriousness and humility that the query suggested there was some fault in his making, that the word or line lacked exactness, clarity, or force. Apart from Pound, the only person who worked on *The Waste Land* was his wife, to whom for obvious reasons he submitted "A Game of Chess." It says much for her that she applauded as wonderful what Pound queried as a too photographic, that is

87

realistic, presentation of a failed marriage relation. He took out, at her request, only one line: "The ivory men make company between us." In the monologue that follows he adopted two lines she supplied, "If you don't like it you can get on with it" and "What you get married for if you don't want to have children." Her ear for cockney was much better than his. But Pound's criticism goes far beyond anything any of Eliot's friends later could attempt, for none of them had Pound's authority. The drafts he has worked over are a unique record of the normal interplay between creation and criticism that results in a poem taking place in two minds instead of in the single mind of the creator-critic.

But in addition to the drafts Pound worked on we have also some of Eliot's own first drafts, some going back a long way. Two of these, which Mrs. Eliot says would seem to have been written in 1914, or even earlier, made their contribution to the fifth part "What the Thunder Said," written at Lausanne, and, as the draft shows, written with extraordinary ease. These early fragments point very clearly to the nature of Eliot's gift: his power over the phrase or line, for lines of startling beauty and originality appear in them; and the fleeting and fragmentary nature of his inspiration, which seems always to have come in jets or spurts, which would last as long as a certain rhythm lasted. A brief early poem, for instance, supplied the first line of "What the Thunder Said" and set up the tune of its first paragraph. In the early poem it is a monotonous tune:

> After the turning of the inspired days
> After the praying and the silence and the crying
> And the inevitable ending of a thousand ways
> And frosty vigil kept in withered gardens

After the life and death of lonely places
After the judges and the advocates and wardens
And the torchlight red on sweaty faces
After the turning of inspired nights
And the shaking spears and flickering lights—
After the living and the dying—
After the ending of this inspiration
And the torches and the faces and the shouting
The world seemed futile—like a Sunday outing.

This tune is beautifully modulated in the passage built upon it:

After the torchlight red on sweaty faces
After the frosty silence in the gardens,
After the agony in stony places
The shouting and the crying
Prison and palace and reverberation
Of thunder of spring over distant mountains
He who was living is now dead
We who were living are now dying
With a little patience.

This ease and freedom when a tune, as it were, held him in its power can be seen in the almost perfectly clean first draft of the passage that follows, the twenty-nine lines of the passage through the waterless mountains followed by the hermit thrush's "water-dripping song," which Eliot thought the best lines in the poem.[13] It can also be seen in the again almost perfectly clean first draft of the

[13] Eliot to Ford Madox Ford (14 August 1923): "There are I think about 30 *good* lines in *The Waste Land*. Can you find them? The rest is ephemeral." (4 October 1923): "As for the lines I mention you need not scratch your head over them. They are the 29 lines of the water-dripping song in the last part." (Correspondence in Cornell University Library.)

song of the Thames daughters, built on the rhythm of
Weiálalá/leiá. This contrasts strikingly with the speeches
of the three daughters, which had to be moulded into
their final moving form. The leaf containing their
speeches is one of the few first drafts on which there are
markings by Pound. Mrs. Eliot says they are in pencil
and green crayon. I should like to know which are which.
The first daughter, the girl from Highbury, was originally
allowed a longish speech, giving her exact social position.
To read it is oddly like moving suddenly from *The Waste
Land* to *The Confidential Clerk*, as the Fresca couplets
anticipate *The Cocktail Party*.

> Highbury bore me. Highbury's children
> Played under green trees and in the dusty Park.
> Mine were humble people and conservative
> As neither the rich nor the working class know.
> My father had a small business, somewhere in the city
> A small business, an anxious business, providing only
> The house in Highbury, and three weeks at [Shanklin]
> > *corrected to* Bognor
> Highbury bore me. Richmond and Kew
> Undid me. At Kew we had tea.
> [At] Near Richmond on the river at last
> [Stretched o] On the floor of a perilous canoe
> I raised my knees.

Eliot crossed this out; but Pound has written against it
"Type this out *anyhow*." Beneath it Eliot has written four
lines which Pound approved as "OK" and "echt":

> Trams and dusty trees.
> Highbury bore me. Richmond and Kew
> Undid me. [Beyond] By Richmond I raised my knees
> Stretched on the floor of a perilous canoe.

90

There is no typescript of this so one cannot tell when
"Supine" replaced "Stretched on" or when the rather risky
word "perilous," which might suggest to the ribald the
danger of copulating in a canoe, was replaced by "nar-
row." The girl who walks the streets at Moorgate then
gave little trouble for the form had been found; but on
the verso of the sheet Eliot had trouble with the girl on
Margate sands: he first wrote two lines "I was to be grate-
ful."/ "There were many others." He then crossed these
out and replaced them with "On Margate sands/ I can
connect" and then went on "Nothing with nothing. He
had." He then crossed out "He had" and wrote a fourth
line "I still feel the pressure of dirty hand." Then the
whole was crossed through, and what remained of the
first three lines was written out below:

> On Margate Sands.
> I can connect
> Nothing with nothing.

The fourth line was transformed into an image:

> The broken finger nails of dirty hands,

and then a phrase was picked up from the cancelled
speech of the girl from Highbury, a phrase that in its final
form has lost its purely social connotation, and places the
girl not in a social class but in the great class of Dostoev-
sky's "poor folk," the "insulted and injured":

> My people [are plain] humble people, who expect
> Nothing.

One sees in Eliot's drafts two things, his natural lyri-
cism on the one hand, and a process by which from a
rather pedestrian passage words, phrases, lines are res-
cued to produce brief concise passages pregnant with
meaning.

The bad passages that Pound cut out and the weak ones he reduced are passages in which Eliot was attempting to write against the natural bent of his genius, trying to keep to a manner and a style over a longer span than was natural to him, and using a tune or rhythm, whether couplets, quatrains, or blank verse, that was not for him a voice of feeling. Much as I enjoy the brilliance and wit of the early poems in quatrain, they are virtuoso performances. I think those critics are right who see them as a kind of aberration, outside the real line of development of Eliot as a poet. For, as well as needing to find images in which feelings could be expressed, or around which feelings could cluster, the famous "objective correlatives," he had also to find a tune expressive of feeling, a rhythm that was as much an "objective correlative" as the image. In fact which came first, rhythm or image, is difficult to say. Eliot himself said in his lecture on *The Music of Poetry* that he knew that "a poem, or a passage of a poem may tend to realize itself first as a particular rhythm before it reaches expression in words, and that this rhythm may bring to birth the idea and the image." When Eliot made up his mind to write a long poem, perhaps urged on by his wife, who was ambitious for his success, as well as by a natural desire to spread his wings and undertake a longer flight, he invented a form that allowed him to compose in the jets and spurts of inspiration that came naturally to him, and, like a worker in mosaic, to find a place in his pattern for lines and even passages that had been composed at very different times. The discovery that poems written separately were beginning to cohere together and could be brought together as the beginning or nucleus of a long poem was a recurring feature of Eliot's career. *The Hollow Men* began with Doris's Dream Songs, *Ash Wednesday* began as three separate poems, and in the final sequence of six their order was altered. *Burnt Norton* was conceived as an independent poem, and itself developed from a passage cut from *Murder in the Cathedral*. It was only during the writing of *East Coker* as a second poem on the model of *Burnt Norton* that the idea of *Four Quartets* took shape. *The Waste Land* differs from these later examples of poems that were not planned but grew. In this case Eliot had decided to write a long poem, and found that poems written long since, fragments, and lines "belonged" to its theme, and would blend, contrast with, and amplify the poem he conceived. But, and I think one must connect this with exhaustion and the flagging inspiration that preceded or possibly precipitated his breakdown, he attempted to fill out his poem and expand it by parodying the styles of other poets, not merely in lines, but in long passages. It is possible he was influenced here by the example of James Joyce in *Ulysses*, and wished his poem to go through English poetic styles as Joyce had gone through English prose styles in the section called "The Oxen of the Sun." For his parodies occur according to an historic scheme. Jacobean dramatists are parodied at the opening of "A Game of Chess," Pope and eighteenth-century narrative poems in quatrain in "The Fire Sermon," and nineteenth-century blank verse, first person, narrative poetry in "Death by Water." This was a false trail. Although Eliot was much addicted to parody I do not think he was a good parodist—his own idiosyncratic voice is too strong to be disguised. Pound rightly saw that the parodies were weak in themselves and also that the tone of the whole poem was too serious to be able to accept extended passages of parody. I think one must assume from its existence in so carefully and neatly written a fair copy that the shipwreck story was written either at

93

Margate or Lausanne, when Eliot took up his poem again, in order to complete the parodic series; but he found his own true voice again composing the close of "The Fire Sermon." And at Lausanne, in what, by his own evidence and the evidence of the drafts, was a single burst of inspiration, he crowned his poem with a last section that matches the beauty of the first and, as it should, transcends it. He discovered in writing this, in the water-dripping passage, a new style, a style that looks forward from *The Waste Land* to *The Hollow Men* and *Ash Wednesday*.[14]

[14] This essay is based on a lecture delivered in the University of Oxford, March 1972.

Robert Langbaum

ONE SIGN of a great poem is that it continues to grow in meaning. A new generation of readers can find in the poem their own preoccupations, and can use those preoccupations to illuminate the poem, to find new meanings in it. Presumably the poem contains the germ of all these accrued meanings; that is why it is great and endures. Certainly no poem ever seemed more of its time than *The Waste Land*, which expressed, as we used to hear, the despair and disillusion of the twenties. Yet a survey of *Waste Land* criticism illustrates perfectly the reciprocal relationship between poem and criticism in the growth, indeed transformation, of a poem's meaning.

The first stunned, admiring critics—Conrad Aiken in 1923, I. A. Richards in 1926—saw the poem as completely incoherent and completely negative in meaning. Richards saw Eliot as "accurately describing the contemporary state of mind . . . by effecting a complete severance between his poetry and *all* beliefs," and remarked "the absence of any coherent intellectual thread upon which the items of the poem are strung." F. R. Leavis (1932) saw in the note on Tiresias a clue to the poem's unity as the unity of "an inclusive consciousness," but saw no progression: "the poem ends where it began." Really constructive criticism begins with F. O. Matthiessen (1935) and continues with such critics as Cleanth Brooks (1939) and George Williamson (1953), who, taking Eliot's notes seriously, find progression, unity, and positive meaning through the built-in analogy with the Grail and vegetation myths. Hugh Kenner (1959) is therefore retrograde in taking off from Pound's later recollection of the original draft as "a series of poems," and in considering that Eliot, dismayed by what he and Pound had wrought through cutting, added the note on Tiresias as an afterthought "to supply the poem with a nameable point of view" that was not really there.[1]

Yet Eliot himself insisted in 1923 that *"The Waste Land* is intended to form a whole."[2] Pound, in his letters of 1921-1922, always referred to *the* poem and showed his sense of its unity by advising Eliot not to omit Phlebas, because "Phlebas is an integral part of the poem; the card

[1] Conrad Aiken, "An Anatomy of Melancholy," *New Republic*, 7 February 1923; I. A. Richards, *Science and Poetry, Principles of Literary Criticism* (London, 1926); F. R. Leavis, *New Bearings in English Poetry* (London, 1932); F. O. Matthiessen, *The Achievement of T. S. Eliot* (New York, 1935); Cleanth Brooks, *Modern Poetry and the Tradition* (Chapel Hill, 1939); George Williamson, *A Reader's Guide to T. S. Eliot* (New York, 1953); Hugh Kenner, *The Invisible Poet: T. S. Eliot* (New York, 1959).

[2] In an autograph letter to L.A.G. Strong, 3 July 1923, quoted in *An Exhibition of Manuscripts and First Editions of T. S. Eliot* (Austin, 1961), p. 10.

pack introduces him, the drowned phoen. sailor."[3] The original draft, now that it has been published, shows Tiresias as we now have him and shows the same organization as the final version.[4] Eliot tried to combine even more disparate fragments than in the final version; Pound cut out the fragments that were at once least successful and most disparate in tone. Even Mr. Kenner refers more than once to "the protagonist," without specifying who he is or how he happens to exist at all in "a series of poems."

The protagonist, Tiresias, and the relation between them present the next problem for *Waste Land* criticism; even the constructive critics have fallen short here. In building upon the work of these critics, I have the advantage of Mr. Kenner's suggestions as to the importance of Bradley and Eliot's doctoral dissertation on Bradley for understanding Eliot's modes of characterization. I have the advantage of the recently published dissertation[5] and of the newly published original draft of *The Waste Land* with Pound's annotations. But my main advantage is the preoccupation of the last decade with problems of identity—a preoccupation that has caused me to single out this question and to try to show that the next step in understanding the structure and meaning of *The Waste Land*, in understanding its continuing greatness and relevance, is to understand that the poem is organized around new concepts of identity and new modes of characterization, concepts and modes that Eliot had been working toward in the poems preceding *The Waste Land.*

[3] *The Letters of Ezra Pound 1907-1941*, ed. D. D. Paige (New York, 1950), [? January] 1922, p. 171.

[4] *The Waste Land: A Facsimile and Transcript of the Original Drafts Including the Annotations of Ezra Pound*, edited with an Introduction by Valerie Eliot (New York, 1971). The draft is part manuscript, part typescript.

[5] *Knowledge and Experience in the Philosophy of F. H. Bradley* (London, 1964).

Prufrock, as we all know by now, takes two aspects of his conscious self ("Let us go then, you and I") to that party where he ought to, but does not, make the sexual proposal that could have saved him. Prufrock's sensuous apprehension reveals also a buried libidinal self that he cannot make operative in the social world, cannot reconcile with the constructed self seen by "The eyes that fix you in a formulated phrase." In the end he makes the split complete by constructing for the regard of his other conscious self a Prufrock as removed as possible from the libidinal self.

> I grow old . . . I grow old . . .
> I shall wear the bottoms of my trousers rolled.

> Shall I part my hair behind? Do I dare to eat
>   a peach?
> I shall wear white flannel trousers, and walk upon
>   the beach.[6]

The timid, sexless old man does, however, walk upon the beach, where—in the final passage that brings to a climax the imagery of ocean (yellow fog, "restaurants with oyster shells") as suggesting sex and unconsciousness—he hears in the sounds of the waves mermaids singing, not to him, but to each other. By relegating his libidinal self to fantasy, Prufrock makes the split wider than ever. He thus avoids sex; he sings his love song to his other conscious self, while the girls sing to each other.

This is Eliot's way of handling character in the early poems. The conscious self is mechanical, constructed, dead; but it has, as its one last sign of vitality, sudden,

[6] Eliot will be quoted from *Collected Poems 1909-1962* (London, 1963).

momentary accesses to a buried libidinal life—accesses
that only deepen the split between unconsciousness and
self-regarding consciousness. Even the utterly blank
young man in the satirical "Portrait of a Lady"—who
puts on "faces" to cover his lack of response to the lady's
advances, just as he keeps his "countenance" before the
miscellaneous, spectacular happenings in the news-
papers—even this emotionally dead young man has mo-
mentary access to a libidinal life recalling at least things
other people have desired:

> I keep my countenance,
> I remain self-possessed
> Except when a street-piano, mechanical and tired
> Reiterates some worn-out common song
> With the smell of hyacinths across the garden
> Recalling things that other people have desired.
> Are these ideas right or wrong?

The pattern, distinctively post-romantic, is to be found
in a poem like Arnold's "The Buried Life." The romanti-
cists portray the conscious self as connected with the un-
conscious and suffused with its vitality. In "The Buried
Life," however, Arnold portrays our conscious existence
as an unenergetic "Eddying at large in blind uncertainty."
"Tricked in disguises, alien to the rest/ Of men, and alien
to themselves," men are cut off from their unconscious
self—except for an inexplicable nostalgia:

> But often, in the world's most crowded streets,
> But often, in the din of strife,
> There rises an unspeakable desire
> After the knowledge of our buried life.

And sometimes, in rare erotic moments, we have access
to our buried self:

99

A bolt is shot back somewhere in our breast,
And a lost pulse of feeling stirs again.
The eye sinks inward, and the heart lies plain,
And what we mean, we say, and what we would, we
    know.
A man becomes aware of his life's flow,
And hears its winding murmur; and he sees
The meadows where it glides, the sun, the breeze.

The buried self is non-individual; it is the life force. It is well that it is buried, for man would with his meddling intellect "well-nigh change his own identity," but is in spite of himself carried, by the unregarded river in his breast, to the fulfillment of his biological destiny and "genuine self."

In Eliot, the self is buried even deeper than in Arnold and is even less individual. The buried self is, in *The Waste Land*, extended in time through unconscious racial memory. When the upper-class lady, aware of inner vacancy, asks: " 'What shall I do now? What shall I do?/ . . . What shall we do tomorrow?/ What shall we ever do?' "—the protagonist answers by describing the routine of their life:

> The hot water at ten.
> And if it rains, a closed car at four.
> And we shall play a game of chess,
> Pressing lidless eyes and waiting for a knock upon
>   the door.

On the surface, his answer confirms her sense of vacancy; we shall fill our lives, he is saying, with meaningless routines. But there is also a positive implication, deriving from the poem's underlying patterns, that these routines are unconscious repetitions of ancient rituals. The morn-

100

ing bath recalls rituals of purification and rebirth through water. The game of chess recalls not only the game played in Middleton's *Women Beware Women* while destiny works itself out behind the door, but also all the games, including the Tarot cards, by which men have tried to foresee and manipulate destiny while waiting for its inevitable arrival. It is the consciousness of the poem blending imperceptibly with the protagonist's consciousness that makes us aware of what the protagonist can only know unconsciously.

As in Arnold's poem, the characters are, in spite of themselves, living their buried life; but they do this not only through personal, but also through racial memory, through unconsciously making rituals even when they think they have abolished all rituals. Similarly, the personal libidinal associations of music and hyacinths in "Portrait of a Lady" become in *The Waste Land* unconscious memories of ancient rituals and myths. The poem's awareness makes us remember consciously what the protagonist, in recalling the Hyacinth garden, remembers unconsciously—that Hyacinth was a fertility god.

When Eliot, in reviewing *Ulysses* for *The Dial* of November 1923, said that Joyce had discovered in the "continuous parallel between contemporaneity and antiquity" a way of giving shape and significance to modern "futility and anarchy," he surely had in mind his own method in *The Waste Land*, published like *Ulysses* the year before and possibly influenced by it since Eliot read the latter part in manuscript in 1921 when he was just beginning *The Waste Land*.[7] This "mythical method," as Eliot called it, allows the writer to be naturalistic, to portray modern chaos, while suggesting through psychological naturalism a continuing buried life that rises irrepressibly

---

[7] See *Facsimile*, Introduction, pp. xx-xxi.

into those shapes which express the primal meeting of mind with nature. Since the parallel with antiquity appears as unconscious memory, it is psychologically justified and cannot be dismissed as mere literary *appliqué*. The parallel is grounded in that conception of mind as shading off into unconsciousness which, having come from romantic literature, was articulated by Freud and Jung and remains still our conception, indeed our experience, of mind. The mythical method gives a doubleness of language to parallel our doubleness (doubleness between the apparent and buried) of consciousness and selfhood.

This doubleness of language reaches a climax at the end of Part I, "The Burial of the Dead," which deals with the sprouting of seed and tubers in spring. In one of the poem's most powerful passages, the protagonist recognizes an old acquaintance; and just as in "Prufrock" we are to infer the small talk at the party, so here we are to infer an ordinary conversation about gardening. But the language tells us what is unconsciously transpiring.

> There I saw one I knew, and stopped him, crying: "Stetson!
> "You who were with me in the ships at Mylae!
> "That corpse you planted last year in your garden,
> "Has it begun to sprout? Will it bloom this year?
> "Or has the sudden frost disturbed its bed?"

The shocking substitution of "corpse" for "seed" reminds us that corpses are a kind of seed, and that this truth was symbolized in the old vegetation rituals. We find gardening satisfying because we unconsciously repeat the ritual by which gods were killed and buried in order that they might sprout anew as vegetation. Even more surprising is the connection of Stetson with the ships at Mylae—the naval battle where the Carthaginians or Phoenicians were

defeated by the Romans. The passage is a haunting rec-
ognition scene in which conscious recognition derives
from unconscious recognition of another life. The protag-
onist unconsciously recognizes his fellow gardener as also
a fellow sailor and Phoenician; for they are devotees of
rebirth, and it was the Phoenician sailors who carried the
Mysteries or vegetation cults around the Mediterranean.

The heavily ironic final lines return us to the modern
situation:

> "Oh keep the Dog far hence, that's friend to men,
> "Or with his nails he'll dig it up again!
> "You! hypocrite lecteur!—mon semblable,—
>   mon frère!"

Instead of Webster's "keep the wolf far thence that's foe
to men" (*White Devil*, V, iv, 113), the friendly Dog (per-
haps, as Cleanth Brooks has suggested, modern humani-
tarianism) is the more likely animal and the more likely
danger. Webster's dirge says it is good for the dead to be
buried, and Eliot tells why—by digging up the corpse,
the Dog would prevent rebirth. But we are all, protago-
nist and hypocrite readers, with our advanced ideas that
cut us off from the natural cycle, engaged in a conspiracy
against fertility and rebirth. So we return to the theme
with which Part I began: "April is the cruellest month,
breeding/ Lilacs out of the dead land"—the fear of sex,
of burying the seed that will sprout.

In *The Waste Land*, the buried life manifests itself
through the unconscious memory of characters from the
past. There is already some reaching toward this method
in "Prufrock," where Prufrock *consciously* thinks he
might have been John the Baptist, Lazarus, Hamlet. But
the emphasis is on the ironical disparity between these
legendary figures and Prufrock's actual character or lack

of character. Prufrock does not in fact fulfill the destinies of these legendary figures. In *The Waste Land*, however, the speakers do in spite of themselves unconsciously fulfill destinies laid out in myth; and their unconscious identification with the legendary figures who have already walked through these destinies gives them the only substantial identity they have.

Compared to the characters in *The Waste Land*, Prufrock, for all his lack of vitality, has the sharp external delineation of characters in, say, Henry James. He has a name (a characterizing one), a social milieu to which he genuinely belongs, a face (we all have our idea of what he looks like, probably like Eliot). Prufrock has—his deliberate trying on of masks is a sign of this—a clear idea of himself. The characters in *The Waste Land*, however, are nameless, faceless, isolated, and have no clear idea of themselves. All they have is a sense of loss and a neural itch, a restless, inchoate desire to recover what has been lost. But in this very minimum of restless aliveness, they repeat the pattern of the Quest. And it is the archetypal Quest pattern, as manifested in the Grail legend, that gives whatever form there is to the protagonist's movement through the poem.

We would not know what to make of the characters were it not for the intrusion of a central consciousness that assimilates them to characters of the past. This is done through the double language of the Stetson passage. The same purpose is accomplished in Part II through shifting references. Part II opens with an opulently old-fashioned blank-verse-style description, not so much of a lady as of her luxurious surroundings. The chair she sits in reminds us of Cleopatra's "burnished throne" and the stately room of Dido's palace, while a picture recalls the rape of Philomela. The shifting references suggest that the lady is seductive, but that she is also, like Cleopatra with Anthony and Dido with Aeneas, one of those who is in the end violated and abandoned by a man. The theme of violation takes over; for the picture shows Philomela's change, after her rape, into a nightingale whose wordless cry rings down through the ages:

> So rudely forced; yet there the nightingale
> Filled all the desert with inviolable voice
> And still she cried, and still the world pursues,
> "Jug Jug" to dirty ears.

The nightingale's *voice*, the story's meaning, is inviolable; but the violation of innocence in the waste land goes on.

When the lady finally speaks, she utters twentieth-century words that her prototypes of the past would not have understood: " ' My nerves are bad to-night. Yes, bad. Stay with me.' " We gather from the passage that the lady is rich, that her house is filled with mementoes of the past which she understands only as frightening ghosts, that the protagonist to whom she speaks is her lover, and that he has in some special modern sense violated her. The violation would seem to lie in his inability to communicate with her:

> "Speak to me. Why do you never speak. Speak.
> "What are you thinking of? What thinking? What?
> "I never know what you are thinking. Think."

The modern situation is unprecedented and meaningless; therein lies the poem's negative impulse. But, deep down, these people are repeating an ancient drama with ancient meanings; therein lies the poem's positive impulse. The shifting references to various ladies of the past evoke the archetype that subsumes them—the archetype already revealed in Part I, where the protagonist has his fortune told by Madame Sosostris. "Here," she said pulling a card from the ancient Tarot deck, "is Belladonna, the Lady of the Rocks,/ The lady of situations." Because all the ladies referred to are Belladonnas, we understand the character of our modern rich lady and the character—in the abrupt shift to a London pub—of the working-class Belladonna who tells a friend of her efforts to steal away the husband of another friend, another Belladonna, who has ruined her health and looks with abortion pills. Beneath the meaningless surface, the underlying tale tells again of violation in the desert—violation of innocence, sex, fertility.

The protagonist's card is "the drowned Phoenician Sailor." This explains not only the Stetson passage, but also the protagonist's reflection after his card has been drawn: "Those are pearls that were his eyes." The line is from Ariel's song in *The Tempest*, addressed to Prince Ferdinand, who thinks his father, the King of Naples, has been drowned. Lines from *The Tempest* keep running through the protagonist's head, because *The Tempest* is a water poem in which all the human characters are sailors, having sailed to the island. Drowning and metamorphosis, the consolation in Ariel's song, relate to drowning and resurrection in the cult of the Phoenician fertility god Adonis (an effigy of the dead Adonis was cast upon the waves, where resurrection was assumed to take place).[8]

Among the other Tarot cards named is "the one-eyed merchant"; he turns up in Part III as the Smyrna merchant who makes the protagonist a homosexual proposition. Eliot in a note (III, 218) explains his method of characterization: "Just as the one-eyed merchant, seller of cur-

[8] Eliot knew Colin Still's interpretation of *The Tempest* as a Mystery ritual of initiation (*Shakespeare's Mystery Play*, London, 1921).

rants, melts into the Phoenician Sailor, and the latter is not wholly distinct from Ferdinand Prince of Naples, so all the women are one woman, and the two sexes meet in Tiresias. What Tiresias *sees*, in fact, is the substance of the poem." The figures either on the Tarot cards, or in some cases frankly imagined by Eliot to be on them, provide the archetypes from which the nameless, faceless modern characters derive identity. Tiresias, not a Tarot figure but the blind hermaphroditic prophet of Greek mythology, appears only once—in the Part III episode about another violated Belladonna, the typist whose mechanical fornication with a clerk leaves her neither a sense of sin nor a memory of pleasure.

The central consciousness, which intruded through the double language of the Stetson passage and the cultural memory of Part II's introductory passage, now takes on the name of Tiresias: "I Tiresias, old man with wrinkled dugs/ Perceived the scene, and foretold the rest." After the scene has been enacted, Tiresias interjects:

> (And I Tiresias have foresuffered all
> Enacted on this same divan or bed;
> I who have sat by Thebes below the wall
> And walked among the lowest of the dead.)

Again we are enabled to understand the contrast between the passionate auspicious fornications of the past and this modern perfunctory performance. Again we are reminded that this scene is nevertheless a *re*enactment. Sexual union was used in the fertility ceremonies to promote by sympathetic magic the fertility of the soil. But modern sexuality is sterile.

Through the Tiresias consciousness in him, the protagonist repeatedly finds an underlying ancient pattern but also sees that in the modern situation the pattern does not

107

come to the preordained conclusion. This gives a direction to his Quest—to complete the pattern by restoring fertility. It is a sign of their connection that Tiresias appears as a stand-in for the protagonist in just the scene the protagonist can only have imagined.

To say that all the characters meet in Tiresias is to suggest that archetypal identities emerge from larger archetypes, in the way smaller Chinese boxes emerge from larger. The Smyrna merchant, identified with the Tarot one-eyed merchant, propositions the protagonist, who is identified with the Phoenician Sailor. Yet we are told that the one-eyed merchant melts into the Phoenician Sailor; so that the protagonist really stands on both sides of the proposition. In the same way the protagonist is identified with the Quester of the Grail legend, who sets out to find the Grail and thus cure the ailing Fisher King and restore fertility to the waste land. The protagonist is the Quester inasmuch as he moves through the episodes of the poem to arrive at the Perilous Chapel. But in the following lines from Part III, he is the Fisher King, whose illness is in some Grail romances assigned to the King's brother or father:

> While I was fishing in the dull canal
> On a winter evening round behind the gashouse
> Musing upon the king my brother's wreck
> And on the king my father's death before him.

He is also—according to the method of shifting references—Prince Ferdinand (from whom, in *Tempest*, I, ii, 390-91, the last two lines derive), Hamlet, Claudius: all of whom have to do with dead kings who in turn recall the murdered kings of vegetation ritual. All this combines with the modern industrial setting to portray the modern moment with modern voices and collapse them into timeless archetypes. At the end of the poem, the protagonist is both Quester and Fisher King; he is the Fisher King questing for a cure: "I sat upon the shore/ Fishing, with the arid plain behind me."

Since the protagonist plays at one and the same time both active and passive roles, we must understand all the characters as aspects or projections of his consciousness—that the poem is essentially a monodrama. It is difficult to say just where the various characters melt into the protagonist and where the protagonist melts into the poet. We have to distinguish the scenes in which the protagonist himself plays a part—the recollection of the Hyacinth garden, the visit to Madame Sosostris, the meeting with Stetson, the scene with the rich Belladonna— from the scenes in the pub and at the typist's. We can either consider that the protagonist overhears the first and imagines the second, or that at these points the poet's consciousness takes leave of the protagonist to portray parallel instances. I prefer the first line of interpretation because it yields a more consistent structure on the model of romantic monodrama. In *Faust* and *Manfred*, the other characters do not have the same order of existence as the protagonists' just because the protagonists' consciousnesses blend with the poets'. We must understand the other characters, therefore, as ambiguously objective, as only partly themselves and partly the projection of forces within the protagonist and ultimately within the poet. If we take the line that Eliot's poem is what the protagonist *sees*, then Tiresias becomes the figure in which the protagonist's consciousness blends perfectly with the poet's so that the protagonist can *see* imaginatively more than he could physically. (Pound in one of his annotations calls Eliot Tiresias.)[9]

[9] *Facsimile*, p. 47.

But the poet's consciousness is itself an aspect of the age's. We get the overheard scraps of conversation, miscellaneous literary tags, and incoherent cultural recollections that would stock a modern cultivated cosmopolitan mind of 1920. This is where Western culture has come to, the poem is telling us, as of 1920. The protagonist's consciousness emerges from the collective consciousness of the time, as another nameless, faceless modern voice. The protagonist has no character in the old-fashioned sense; for he acquires delineation or identity not through individualization, but through making connection with ancient archetypes.

The point is that Eliot introduces a new method of characterization deriving from the reaction against the nineteenth-century belief in the individual as the one reality you could be sure of. Eliot's nameless, faceless voices derive from the twentieth-century sense that the self, if it exists at all, is changing and discontinuous, and that its unity is as problematical as its freedom from external conditions. In *The Waste Land*, and in his earlier poems, Eliot is preoccupied with the mechanical, automatic quality of existence. In "Rhapsody on a Windy Night," he had written:

> I could see nothing behind that child's eye.
> I have seen eyes in the street
> Trying to peer through lighted shutters,
> And a crab one afternoon in a pool,
> An old crab with barnacles on his back,
> Gripped the end of a stick which I held him.

In *The Waste Land*, he says of the clerk: "Exploring hands encounter no defence"; and of the typist afterward: "She smoothes her hair with automatic hand,/ And puts a record on the gramophone." The solution, toward

110

which he had been finding his way through the early poems, is the breaking out from and enlargement of self through archetypalization. Behind the solution lie the demonstrations by Freud and Jung that when we delve deep into the psyche we find an archetypal self and a desire to repeat the patterns laid out in the sort of myths described by Frazer and Jessie Weston.

The Waste Land opens with scraps of cosmopolitan conversations that the protagonist might be understood to overhear, but which have enough in common to project an upper-class tourist mentality, out of touch with and afraid of life's rhythms: "I read, much of the night, and go south in the winter"—yet still feeding on recollected moments of genuine experience:

> And when we were children, staying at the arch-duke's,
> My cousin's, he took me out on a sled,
> And I was frightened. He said, Marie,
> Marie, hold on tight. And down we went.
> In the mountains, there you feel free.

There follow cultural recollections, mainly from the Bible—"I will show you fear in a handful of dust"—that establish in the image of the dry waste land the spiritual habitat of the previous speakers. This is a new prophetic voice, the Tiresias consciousness, which goes on through a recollection of the Sailor's song that opens Wagner's *Tristan* to establish also the opposite Sailor theme of water and hope for redemption. There follows a personal memory of love; and only here, in the lines introduced by a dash, can we single out a voice that we come to recognize as the protagonist's.

111

> "You gave me hyacinths first a year ago;
> "They called me the hyacinth girl."
> —Yet when we came back, late, from the
>   Hyacinth garden,
> Your arms full, and your hair wet, I could not
> Speak, and my eyes failed, I was neither
> Living nor dead, and I knew nothing,
> Looking into the heart of light, the silence.
> *Oed' und leer das Meer.*

The protagonist had in the past his chance for love; he had like Marie his perfect moment, his vision of fulfillment. But he was unable to reach out and take what the moment offered, and thus break through to fertility, creativity. We know he failed only through the last line from the opening of Wagner's tragic Third Act: "Desolate and empty the sea."

This way of rendering the protagonist's failure makes it also collective; as does the reference to the Hyacinth garden, since Hyacinth was a fertility god. (Eliot capitalized the small *h* of the original draft; but restored it for the final edition of 1963, having presumably lost interest by then in vegetation myths.) It is the vision and loss of vision that sets the protagonist in motion; insofar as *The Waste Land* has a plot, it tells the story of the protagonist's attempt to recover his lost vision. All his subsequent memories are transformations of the scene in the Hyacinth garden. This observation is confirmed by the words, which I have bracketed, that Eliot deleted from the original draft. When in Part II the rich lady asks: " 'Do you remember/ Nothing?' "—the protagonist answers: "I remember/ [The hyacinth garden.] Those are pearls that were his eyes [,yes!]" The Hyacinth garden (love) and Ariel's song (drowning) are related as forms of natural salvation (love is a kind of drowning). This attempt at recovery is the pattern of the Grail Quest; in most versions, a vision or fleeting sight of the Grail leads to the Quest to recover the Grail.

The Waste Land is about sexual failure as a sign of spiritual failure. This is made especially clear by the deleted opening passage about a rowdy Irishman, on an all-night binge, who lands in a brothel but is too drunk to have intercourse. The original draft then shifts to "April is the cruellest month"—about upper-class people who, like the Irishman, fail in sex not because they are practicing Christian abstinence but because of spiritual torpor. The vegetation myths are better than Christianity for diagnosing modern sexual failure; for the myths make clear that sex and religion spring from the same impulse and that sexual and religious fulfillment are related.

To understand how far Eliot has come in his treatment of sex and in his concepts of character and identity, we have only to compare the memory of the Hyacinth garden with a corresponding memory in the early poem, written in French, "Dans le Restaurant." In the French poem, a dirty broken-down waiter recalls an amorous experience under a tree in the rain when he was only seven and the little girl was even younger. She was soaking wet, he gave her primroses and tickled her to make her laugh. He experienced a moment of power and ecstasy. But he too lost his vision, for a big dog came along and he became scared and deserted her; he has never fulfilled the promise of that moment. The customer to whom he has insisted on telling this story remarks on his physical filthiness as a way of separating the waiter from himself: "What right have you to experiences like mine?" The customer gives the waiter ten sous for a bath.

The poem escapes from this sordid situation by taking

a quite unprepared-for leap to the cleansing by drowning of Phlebas the Phoenician, a character for whom we have not been in the least prepared.

> Phlébas, le Phénicien, pendant quinze jours noyé,
> Oubliait les cris des mouettes et la houle de Cornouaille,
> Et les profits et les pertes. . . .

The sudden contrast affords welcome relief. Since Part IV of *The Waste Land* is an English revision of this passage:

> Phlebas the Phoenician, a fortnight dead,
> Forgot the cry of gulls, and the deep sea swell
> And the profit and loss,

we are justified in connecting certain details preceding this passage with "Dans le Restaurant." The dog may stand behind " 'Oh keep the Dog far hence,' " and the customer who wants to separate himself from the waiter may stand behind " 'You! hypocrite lecteur!—mon semblable,—mon frère!' " But most important, the connection with the waiter's memory suggests that the protagonist betrayed the hyacinth girl through non-consummation. The experience took place *after* "we came back, late, from the Hyacinth garden," presumably in the rooms of one or the other. In both scenes, sexuality is associated with rain and flowers; the hyacinth girl came back with her arms full of flowers and her hair wet.

Having failed to consummate a union that would have combined love with sex, the protagonist turns to the fortune-teller and then proceeds to live out his fortune by experiencing dry, sterile lust. He fails the rich Belladonna, overhears the dialogue in the pub, is propositioned by the Smyrna merchant, conceives the typist's fornication and the lament of the girl seduced on the Thames:

> "Highbury bore me. Richmond and Kew
> Undid me. By Richmond I raised my knees
> Supine on the floor of a narrow canoe."

Finally the imagery of dryness and burning comes to a climax: "Burning burning burning burning," and we are afforded the welcome relief of Phlebas's "Death By Water."

> A current under sea
> Picked his bones in whispers. As he rose and fell
> He passed the stages of his age and youth
> Entering the whirlpool.

The passage holds out to the protagonist the possibility of a natural or pagan salvation, the kind suggested by the song from *The Tempest* in which Ariel makes drowning seem so desirable because it is "a sea change/ Into something rich and strange" (I, ii, 401-02).

"Fear death by water," said Madame Sosostris. "Here, said she,/ Is your card, the drowned Phoenician Sailor"; at which point the protagonist recalled "Those are pearls that were his eyes," another line from this same song of Ariel's. Thus Eliot does in *The Waste Land* what he has not done in "Dans le Restaurant": he prepares for the drowning of Phlebas. He retains on the surface the vacant characters of the earlier poem, but he prepares beneath the surface archetypal identities that give the characters positive force. We must read the protagonist's development in self-understanding through the shift in the archetypes with which he identifies himself. In identifying himself with Phlebas, the protagonist fulfills in Part IV his natural fortune. Part V, "What the Thunder Said," moves beyond Madame Sosostris, who could not find the "Hanged Man." Part V explores the possibility of a super-

115

natural answer through the unpredictable miracle of revelation.

The drowning of Phlebas must be understood as the equivalent of a psychological experience—as a *rite de passage* or psychic dying through which the protagonist can be reborn into the identity that enables him to continue his Quest. The protagonist has after Part IV outgrown pagan archetypes; the references now are to Christianity and the higher ethical Hinduism of the Upanishads. The Hyacinth garden turns into the garden of Gethsemane: "After the torchlight red on sweaty faces/ After the frosty silence in the gardens." The missing "Hanged Man" of the Tarot deck turns into the hooded figure whom the disciples on the journey to Emmaus saw but did not recognize as the risen Christ:

> Who is the third who walks always beside you?
> When I count, there are only you and I together
> But when I look ahead up the white road
> There is always another one walking beside you
> Gliding wrapt in a brown mantle, hooded
> I do not know whether a man or a woman
> —But who is that on the other side of you?

Eliot so suggestively avoids specification that he eludes an exclusively Christian reading and turns the personages and situation archetypal. He makes the passage refer also to an account he read of an Antarctic expedition where the explorers, as he says in his note to these lines, "at the extremity of their strength, had the constant delusion that there was *one more member* than could actually be counted." Because of the new concept of identity advanced in *The Waste Land*, we have had to learn how to read a passage in which the twentieth-century London protagonist exhibits his character by melting into other

quite remote characters—a disciple of Christ, an Ant-
arctic explorer. We are to understand by the identifica-
tions that the protagonist has reached the point where he
has intimations of Godhead.

It is in Part v that the Grail legend becomes most ex-
plicit, and explicit in its Christian interpretation. The
protagonist might be said to repeat in his own progress
the evolution of the Grail legend, as described by Jessie
Weston, from pagan ritual to Christian romance.[10] Even
those female lamentations which precede the protago-
nist's arrival at the empty chapel—and which refer, as
Eliot's note explains, to "the present decay of eastern
Europe"—recall the lamenting voices of unseen women
that, in certain versions described by Miss Weston, the
Grail knight hears amid the desolation of the Perilous
Chapel. When in the final passage the protagonist be-
comes both Quester and Fisher King, there is a powerful
recapitulation of the disorder that has been the poem's
main theme. We are given a most poignant sense of the
incoherent fragments that stock the cultural memory of
Europe.

> I sat upon the shore
> Fishing, with the arid plain behind me
> Shall I at least set my lands in order?
> London Bridge is falling down falling down falling down
> *Poi s'ascose nel foco che gli affina*
> *Quando fiam uti chelidon*—O swallow swallow
> *Le Prince d'Aquitaine à la tour abolie*
> These fragments I have shored against my ruins
> Why then Ile fit you. Hieronymo's mad againe.
> Datta. Dayadhvam. Damyata.
> Shantih   shantih   shantih.

[10] *From Ritual to Romance* (Cambridge, 1920).

117

Yet all these apparently miscellaneous fragments speak of purgation—whether through the refining fire of Dante's line, or the melancholy of Nerval's ghostly Prince, or the purposeful madness of Kyd's Hieronymo—or else they speak of desire for salvation, as in the line from the Latin *Pervigilium Veneris*: "When shall I become as the swallow?"

"These fragments I have shored against my ruins." The line turns to a positive purpose the fragmentation upon which the poem has been built. They point to a tradition which, though in disarray, is all we have to draw on for salvation. The fragments are in many languages because all European culture is being tapped, going back to its earliest origins in the Sanskrit Upanishads. As the protagonist, through association and memory, makes his identity, he is able to give the fragments a new order. They are made to issue in the three Sanskrit precepts—give, sympathize, control—upon which the protagonist has already meditated, and which are to guide him toward that peace, signified by *shantih*, which passes understanding.

Once we see that *The Waste Land* dramatizes the making of an identity, that the Quest is for personal order that leads to cultural order and cultural order that leads to personal order, then the poem turns out more positive than we used to think it. The deadness and disorder that made the biggest, indeed the only, impression on the poem's first readers are seen as a phase through which the poem passes to point toward the Christian poems that are to follow Eliot's conversion in 1927. We can now see from *The Waste Land* that Eliot was by 1922 farther along toward conversion than we had thought. Eliot— "Fishing, with the arid plain behind me," and wanting to set "my lands in order"—has by now put behind him all liberal humanitarian modern answers: he is fishing, waiting for revelation. He has by now seen the need for Christianity, though he still cannot believe.

To understand the modern problem of identity that Eliot is trying to solve in *The Waste Land*, we have to look back not to "Prufrock" or "Portrait of a Lady," whose speakers are still, as I have suggested, Jamesian in their delineation, but to "Preludes" and "Rhapsody on a Windy Night," which were written during those same years, 1909-1911. The characters of these poems are not, like Prufrock and the lady, separated from external reality by an unspoken ideal; they are, on the contrary, undistinguishable from the images of external reality that make up their consciousness.

II

The morning comes to consciousness
Of faint stale smells of beer . . .

III

You dozed, and watched the night revealing
The thousand sordid images
Of which your soul was constituted;
They flickered against the ceiling.
And when all the world came back
And the light crept up between the shutters
And you heard the sparrows in the gutters,
You had such a vision of the street
As the street hardly understands; . . .

IV

His soul stretched tight across the skies
That fade behind a city block,
Or trampled by insistent feet
At four and five and six o'clock.

119

In all these instances from "Preludes," there is a minimum of that distinction between perceiver and perceived, and hence of that will and organizing power, which constitute an identity. Yet the validity of the sensations and the vision of the street suggest some minimal awareness.

"Rhapsody on a Windy Night" parodies the Wordsworth tradition in that it opens up, under the transforming influence of moonlight, the flow of memory and association. But moonlight in an urban setting does not yield beauty. Reinforced by the light of a street lamp, it transforms the streetwalker into a grotesque:

> "Regard that woman
> Who hesitates toward you in the light of the door
> Which opens on her like a grin.
> You see the border of her dress
> Is torn and stained with sand,
> And you see the corner of her eye
> Twists like a crooked pin."

The twisted eye recalls the memory of twisted things:

> The memory throws up high and dry
> A crowd of twisted things;
> A twisted branch upon the beach . . .
> A broken spring in a factory yard,
> Rust that clings to the form that the strength has left
> Hard and curled and ready to snap.

Perception again stirs memory when the sight of a cat slipping out its tongue to devour butter recalls, in the passage I have quoted earlier, the equally automatic reach of a child's hand for a toy: "I could see nothing behind that child's eye."

This vacancy, this automatic action without reserve of

thought and feeling, fascinates Eliot in his early view of character. Prufrock, who is paralyzed by too much reserve of thought and feeling, longs for such automatism: "I should have been a pair of ragged claws." But the speaker of "Preludes" sees it as wiping out individuality. "The morning comes to consciousness" means there is no distinction among all the people who come to minimal consciousness because it is morning:

> One thinks of all the hands
> That are raising dingy shades
> In a thousand furnished rooms.

In "Preludes" IV, the soul of the clerk returning from work at evening is trampled like the street "by insistent feet." His soul is also "stretched tight across the skies," suggesting perhaps his taut nerves.

> And short square fingers stuffing pipes,
> And evening newspapers, and eyes
> Assured of certain certainties,
> The conscience of a blackened street
> Impatient to assume the world.

The certainties of such people, certainties derived from the mass media and from urban sensations, are as determined and insensitive as the street blackened by trampling. Their certainties are almost as automatic as the grasping reflex of the crab in "Rhapsody."

In "Rhapsody," the speaker on his way home late at night recognizes the number on his door. " 'Memory!' " says the street lamp sardonically, contrasting the mechanical memory of one's address with Wordsworthian memory. The indoor lamp " 'spreads a ring on the stair,' " giving another kind of light from the moon's.

"Mount.
The bed is open; the tooth-brush hangs on the wall,
Put your shoes at the door, sleep, prepare for life."

The last twist of the knife.

If the moonlight has yielded such mechanical sensations and memories, what can be expected of ordinary life? The speaker's thoughts are given to him by the street lamps—a sign that perceiver and perceived are not distinguished.

The view of the self in these two poems was either influenced by Bradley, or else, what is more likely, Bradley confirmed for Eliot a view of the self he had already arrived at on his own.[11] F. H. Bradley, the turn-of-the-century English philosopher, taught that the self can be known only through experience; for the self cannot be distinguished from its psychical contents, its sensations and memories of sensations. For the same reason, the self is in experience hardly distinguishable from the not-self—each fills and determines the other. "We have no right, except in the most provisional way," says Eliot in explaining Bradley, "to speak of *my* experience, since the I is a construction out of experience, an abstraction from it."[12] Bradley speaks, therefore, not of subjective perceivers but of subjective-objective centers of experience— "finite centres." There are as many universes as there are finite centres; for as Bradley puts it: "My external sensations are no less private to myself than are my thoughts or my feelings. In either case my experience falls within my own circle, a circle closed on the outside; and, with

[11] We do not know when Eliot first read Bradley, but he did not begin to study him until he returned from Paris to Harvard in autumn 1911 to work for a doctorate in philosophy.
[12] *Knowledge and Experience*, p. 19.

all its elements alike, every sphere is opaque to the others which surround it. . . . In brief, regarded as an existence which appears in a soul, the whole world for each is peculiar and private to that soul." Eliot quotes this passage in a note to lines v, 411-13 of *The Waste Land*— lines in which the self as so described is the thing to be overcome. Through an analogy to the prison in which Dante's Count Ugolino was locked up to starve to death, Eliot, in meditating on the Sanskrit precept *Dayadhvam* (sympathize), is saying we must break out of the Bradleyan prisonhouse of self.

In "Preludes" and "Rhapsody," the Bradleyan view of self as opaque and discontinuous ("The usual self of one period is not the usual self of another")[13] is presented as true but awful. In both poems, the word *I* is severely repressed. But we can tell from the perceived details that the *speakers*—as distinguished from the characters they perceive—have in reserve an unacknowledged ideal by which they judge the mechanical life they portray. In "Preludes," the speaker finally uses *I* to express through the trampled souls on trampled streets an accumulating sense of violation, and to suggest that even these mechanical registers of sensation may obscurely feel some core of self that has been violated.

> I am moved by fancies that are curled
> Around these images, and cling:
> The notion of some infinitely gentle
> Infinitely suffering thing.

But no, this is only fancy; the universe is as sordid and meaningless as the urban scene:

[13] *Appearance and Reality*, 2nd ed. (London, 1902), pp. 346, 79.

> Wipe your hand across your mouth, and laugh;
> The worlds revolve like ancient women
> Gathering fuel in vacant lots.

Yet the fancy of some other possibility remains with us here and in "Rhapsody."

Having dissolved the distinction between subject and object, Bradley himself acknowledges a "limit of this interchange of content between the not-self and the self." He admits that we do nevertheless entertain obscure "sensations of an essential selfhood," which derive from "our ability to feel a discrepancy between our felt self and any object before it. This . . . gives us the idea of an unreduced residue."[14] It is out of this unreduced residue, sensed in spite of the problematical nature of the self, that modern literature generates the mysteries of identity. And it is this unreduced residue—sensed as a mere perceptual bias in "Preludes" and "Rhapsody," and in the blank young man in "Portrait" who responds to the street piano and the smell of hyacinths—that develops into a positive force in *The Waste Land*.

The structure of "Preludes" anticipates that of *The Waste Land*. Both present separate vignettes of city life; yet the vignettes are unified by the central consciousness which must be understood as perceiving or imagining them all. The speaker of "Preludes," having thought of all the morning hands "raising dingy shades/ In a thousand furnished rooms," imagines himself in the furnished room where the streetwalker wakes up alone. In the same way, the protagonist of *The Waste Land* imagines himself at evening in the furnished room where the typist receives the clerk; and he does this after envisioning the city's taut nerves at the end of a working day:

[14] *Appearance and Reality*, pp. 92-93.

124

At the violet hour, when the eyes and back
Turn upward from the desk, when the human engine waits
Like a taxi throbbing waiting.

Not rest but stimulation is wanted (in the original draft, the next line was: "To spring to pleasure through the horn or ivory gate"); hence the intercourse that turns out as mechanical as the throbbing. This typist and clerk, too, have had their souls trampled by the "insistent feet" returning from work.

"Preludes" gives us a world where people live alone in furnished rooms; the speaker of "Rhapsody" returns to such a room. *The Waste Land* gives us a world in which people do not communicate. Dialogues are one-sided; the answer, when there is an answer, is thought rather than spoken and does not answer the question:

> "Speak to me. Why do you never speak. Speak.
> "What are you thinking of?" . . .

> I think we are in rats' alley
> Where the dead men lost their bones.

But this isolation is counteracted by the ability of the speaker in "Preludes" and the protagonist in *The Waste Land* to project into the other characters. Hence the speaker's fancy in "Preludes" is of a compassionate humanity they all share, and his view remains general when he reverses himself to see that our general fate, instead, is as loveless as the force that moves the stars. The final lines may invoke an ironical comparison with Dante's final vision in *Paradiso* of "Love that moves the sun and the other stars." And, indeed, the minimal "notion of some infinitely gentle/ Infinitely suffering thing" is just the unreduced residue of feeling out of which Christian mythology takes shape.

In *The Waste Land*, the speaker's projection into the typist's room takes shape in the figure of Tiresias. Bound up with the original draft of *The Waste Land* are some poems that demonstrate the projective sensibility that was to produce Tiresias. In "The death of Saint Narcissus," the speaker knows he has been a tree, a fish, "a young girl/ Caught in the woods by a drunken old man"; now he is happy to experience even martyrdom. "Song. [For the Opherion]" speaks of "Bleeding between two lives"; and some untitled lines help us understand how the protagonist of *The Waste Land* can be both Quester and Fisher King:

> I am the Resurrection and the Life
> I am the things that stay, and those that flow.
> I am the husband and the wife
> And the victim and the sacrificial knife.

The protagonist's projective imagination, which sees or creates the connections among the characters, sees in them a memory of and yearning for a communal identity, and that communal identity is expressed through the mythical figures in the poem, most notably the figures of the Tarot cards. In a 1916 paper, "Leibniz' Monads and Bradley's Finite Centres," Eliot threw light on the method of establishing identities he was to use in *The Waste Land*: "Nothing is real, except experience present in finite centres. The world, for Bradley, is simply the *intending* of a world by several souls or centres. . . . For Bradley, I take it, an object is a common intention of several souls, cut out (as in a sense are the souls themselves) from immediate experience. The genesis of the common world can only be described by admitted fictions."[15]

[15] Reprinted as Appendix in *Knowledge and Experience*, pp. 203-04.

126

Thus the mythical figures and patterns—the Grail Quest, the vegetation myths leading to the Christian myth—are the admitted fictions rising out of the characters' memories and desires, their unreduced residue of feeling. The vision encountered and lost of the hyacinth girl leads to a desire for recovery expressed through the fiction of the Quest. The longing everyone has for water recalls the seasonal alternation of drought and rain; while winter and spring are recalled by the longing for death that leads in the end to the longing for rebirth. The whole connection of human emotions with the cycle of the seasons is expressed through the fictions of the vegetation myths.

The sense of violation we detected in "Preludes" permeates the first three parts of *The Waste Land*. The theme is established through the fiction, represented in the rich Belladonna's painting, of Philomela's rape; and that fiction applies to all the women in the poem, including such recollected victims as Dante's La Pia and Ophelia (III, 293-94, 306). The Christian imagery of Part v makes explicit our accumulating sense that all the violations come together in the figure of Jesus, the arch-victim.

The movement from the fire of Part III to the relief, in Part IV, through water prepares the sensuous texture out of which, in Part v, the figures of Jesus and other redeemers take shape. They take shape because the senses require them to take shape, the senses as objective correlatives to the protagonist's emotions:

> Ganga was sunken, and the limp leaves
> Waited for rain, while the black clouds
> Gathered far distant, over Himavant.
> The jungle crouched, humped in silence.
> Then spoke the thunder.

127

Earlier, a similar rendition of thirst gives rise to the figure of Jesus:

> If there were the sound of water only
> Not the cicada
> And dry grass singing
> But sound of water over a rock
> Where the hermit-thrush sings in the pine trees
> Drip drop drip drop drop drop drop
> But there is no water.

The longing for water, for even the sound of water, together with the hope offered by the lovely water-dripping song of the hermit-thrush, leads to "Who is the third?" The third, as we have seen, is the unrecognized apparition born of the Antarctic explorers' despair, and the unrecognized apparition of Jesus born of the disciples' grief over the Crucifixion. In both cases the apparition was delivering. *The Waste Land*'s positive force derives from the characters' ability to generate, from an unreduced residue of feeling, an archetypal identity which delivers them from the closed circle of the Bradleyan self and the immediate historical moment.

Robert M.
Adams

PRECIPITATING ELIOT

". . . I have, I pride myself, kept abreast of the times in literature; at least, if I have not, the times have moved very speedily indeed."—Letter signed Helen B. Trundlett, Batton, Kent, *The Egoist*, December 1917

A SMALL, ironic, and perhaps extraneous circumstance provides a first surface for reflection. Writing a paper on T. S. Eliot in 1972 is easier, on at least one preliminary level, than it ever used to be. There are all sorts of books and articles on the topic: they are all on the shelves. There is a way of saying this that makes the remark sound malignant and triumphant; I mean no such tone to be heard. It is an occasion for surprise only because, for almost forty years, I have been accustomed to find a snarl of students buzzing over and about books by and about T. S. Eliot. The books are still there, in greater numbers than ever; but the students, like Eliot personae, "departed have left no addresses." To anyone of my vintage, the change is particularly shocking because, as I look back over my own education, which was typical of its era, it seems to have been soaked in an awareness of Eliot, to have been controlled by his terminology, his tonality, his awareness of what he called, no doubt over-magisterially, "tradition"—that is, styles of poetry bearing affinity to that for which he wished to win a hearing. I will not say that, even

129

in those distant days, we were not aware of anomalies and discords in our feelings about Eliot—some of which can be simply suggested by noting that we first encountered "East Coker" and "The Dry Salvages" in the pages of *Partisan Review*, where, to say the least of it, they made strange dialectic with their near neighbors.[1] Still, there is no point pretending now to have been wiser than we were then; Eliot imposed himself on the literary conscience of my generation in a way, and to a degree, that is only now, with the passage of time, becoming clear. Thus, between a lingering sense of gratitude for insights given, used, and by now adapted into the full structure of our conscious/ unconsciousness, and resentment at having been sometimes imposed on by some formula or phrase that now reveals itself as empty or specious, striking a balance is bound to involve a disturbing little element of self-definition, if such were needed to keep us from feeling privileged in any way.

When Eliot imposed himself and his values emphatically on English literature (and I am not in any way talking about this as an imposition, far less as an imposture), it was of set purpose and in the name of explicit modernity. We hear again and again in his early criticism of "modern" and "contemporary" writing, of certain "tasks" imposed by the times to be completed by writers of "the present." We learn, more authoritatively, of "four or five

---

[1] "East Coker" rubbed elbows with a polemic by Philip Rahv on varieties of Marxist revisionism; "The Dry Salvages" stood directly before James Burnham on the managerial revolution and Dwight Macdonald on the end of capitalism in Germany. It is true that something of the same incongruity could have been found in the pages of *Criterion*, where Eliot, simply to represent the modern temper, was bound to print Marxist authors of whose first premises he disapproved—however he might salve his conscience with the curiously superficial afterthought that Marxists and Christians were both men of principle, "worthy adversaries."

men who count," of the need for "ceaseless employment of criticism by men who are engaged in creative work"— the latter phrase evidently serving to define the former. We hear of the forces of deterioration (a large crawling mass) and of the forces of development (half a dozen men). I am not forcing the cliché if I say that for Eliot, in those early days, the arts frequently stood at the crossroads. "The intelligence of a nation must go on developing," he wrote; "and . . . every writer who does not help develop the language is to the extent to which he is read a positive agent of deterioration."[2] In other words, he who is not with us (the four or five men who count, the half dozen on whom further "development" depends) is against us, thus part of the large crawling mass. Though the quotations are from 1918, the alternatives they pose are stark enough to justify Mr. Bateson's reference, rather approving than otherwise, to "a short reign of terror"[3] necessary to achieve the glorious victory of the early 1920's; certainly in conjunction with the ferocities of Pound and Lewis, they make that phrase inevitable.

Obviously, my generation was not terrorized by Eliot, nor by Ezra Pound either, for that matter. We were persuaded as people are persuaded in this world—half logically, half emotionally, by charm, wit, eloquence, assurance, the obvious presence of enormous talent, fresh learning, and deep concern for letters. We were perhaps awed and partly overawed; and not just by Eliot and Pound, but by the ancient and horrible tradition of critical incomprehension before something new in the arts. It is a terrible old tradition, and almost any attitude, however weak-kneed, is probably preferable to it. Who wants to get himself into the textbooks alongside Jeffreys,

[2] "Observations," *Egoist*, v, 5 (May 1918), pp. 69-70.
[3] *Essays in Criticism*, iii, 1 (January 1953), p. 2.

Croker, and that melancholy mossback who saw in "Pru-
frock" only shameful babblings like those of a drunken
helot? More even than by the subtlety and coherence of
Eliot's position (which started to come under counter-
attack more than twenty years ago), we were persuaded
by the flatulence and scrappiness of the alternatives,
the obvious vulnerability of the assailants. Long after it
was clear that much of what Eliot had advanced during
the years of the First War and during the 1920's was no
longer "modern" or compatible with fresh ways of feel-
ing, his prestige persisted, *faute de mieux*—because most
of the alternatives were less modern, as well as less liber-
ating, than what they offered to replace. As late as the
1950's, for example, Graham Hough, after denouncing
Eliot, Joyce, and Pound with real sharpness and insight,
offered to replace Eliot's image of the poet as a catalyst
mediating between the weight of tradition and the urgent
present, with a Wordsworthian formula, that the poet is
a man speaking to men.[4] Well, of course he is, some-
times; but the implication of this formula, in cutting
down the poet to a more or less successful message-de-
liverer, simply cannot be accepted, it is too restrictive
to be tolerable. The poet may well be a man speaking to
specially prepared or qualified men—and suddenly we
are back with Eliot's tradition, or some variant of it.

Eliot's literary dictatorship, if such it was, commanded
a broad basis of consent because it was beautifully
adapted to the circumstances of its time. Like Dryden's
very similar dictatorship, it combined skepticism and as-
surance in an art of elegant intellectual fence that pro-
tected it against almost any assailant except time. For

[4] *Image and Experience* (London, Duckworth, 1960), "Reflec-
tions on a Literary Revolution," p. 83.

132

thirty or forty years it floated in an atmosphere that reconciled or minimized its anomalies. The structure of assumptions and values was accepted widely and as a whole—because of its merits, yes, but also because those merits suited perfectly the spirit of the age.

Things are of course very different now. Apart from Eliot's social attitudes, which never had much appeal to begin with and rapidly became downright repellent as a result of the Second War, the critical formulae have unravelled fastest. The dissociated sensibility came under open attack in the early 1950's, as an unjustified application to literary history of a concept kidnapped from Remy de Gourmont. So far as I know, formal assaults of equivalent authority have not been mounted against associated doctrines, like that of the objective correlative (which simply got tired and wore out), like the role of tradition and the impersonality of the poet, the notion of a hard, dry, classical literature, or the deprecation of thought as an ingredient of poetry. But these formulae have largely faded from the common critical vocabulary—as if, the Georgian Anthology having been laid to rest and Edmund Gosse routed from the field, their work were done. Gently, regretfully, firmly, Eliot himself withdrew from behind them in his 1961 essay, "To Criticize the Critic."[5] Seen now against the background of Victorian poetic diction, as critical expressions of that impulse which led both Pound and Eliot into a temporary discipleship to Théophile Gautier, the polemical and destructive purpose of these critical doctrines is perfectly clear. As Mr. Hough has already made evident, it was a stylistic revolution that the American cousins set in motion; it involved very

[5] Reprinted under that title in a 1965 volume by Farrar, Straus and Giroux, New York.

little in the way of a new view of man or the cosmos. Neither Pound nor Eliot ever pretended to any such mantic function. As early as 1917, Eliot was saying with some ironic asperity, "Each of us, even the most gifted, can find room in his brain for hardly more than two or three new ideas, or ideas so perfectly assimilated as to be original; for an idea is a specialty, and no one has time for more than a few. . . . In literature especially, the innovations which we can consciously and collectively aim to introduce are few, and mostly technical."[6] Our problem in deciding how much of a revolution Pound and Eliot set in motion was evidently their problem too. Did the development of "the intelligence of a nation" depend on the solving of two or three mostly technical problems by four or five *littérateurs*? Why did these innovations, if they were so slight, require forty or fifty years to work out their implications? Yet if they were more than that, how shall we define that more?

Some ingredients of the problem have already started to precipitate out. If it was not a new way of seeing "man," Eliot's revolution was at least a new way of seeing man's past: his "modernism" was strikingly historical, shaped in its first formulation by the need to displace a shopworn literary heritage (the Georgian Anthology took, perhaps, more knocks from Pound and Eliot than it deserved, acting as a scapegoat for the Victorian age from which it had not broken sharply enough), presided over in its cradle by a miscellany of godfathers and tutelary spirits out of the immediate and remote past. The successive arrival and occasional departure of these literary prototypes has a rhythm of its own—Laforgue and

[6] "Reflections on Contemporary Poetry," *Egoist*, IV, 10 (November 1917).

Dante, Gautier and Gourmont, Baudelaire and Jean de Bosschère, the Jacobean dramatists, Donne, Marvell— not to mention more indirect sources of moral or technical stiffening, like Dostoevsky, Flaubert, Henry James. Perfunctory as it is in my making of it, the list is an impressive one; it could easily be doubled. No other poet in the history of the language, with the possible exception of Pound, has revalued so many reputations, or domesticated so many foreign poets in English taste. In accepting Eliot as my generation did, wholesale, we accepted not only "Prufrock" and *The Sacred Wood*, but an attitude toward the entire European past, a modification of its "pastness," and a spirit of inquiry that seemed to us life-giving. Perhaps that was only one of his two or three ideas, but it was a big one—too big, the critics now seem to feel, to have been expressed with full success in Eliot's first go at expressing it ("Tradition and the Individual Talent");[7] but with the passing of the years, it has been worked out to really enriching and liberating conclusions.

We are bound to be impeded in identifying Eliot's modernism by the turbid circumstance that we live in a medium of his making; the frame of discourse in which we try to place him is largely of his own creation. Still, the precipitation of Eliot has already begun; the water is clearing. When we straighten out some of the ambiguities of that deceitful term "modern," as it applies to Eliot in 1922 and to us in 1972, we may put ourselves in a position to do without it altogether, and then to hazard a guess about the overall shape that literary history may be prepared to see in the Eliot career. Such at least is the plan.

[7] See, for a particularly telling critique of Eliot's use of the word "tradition," Graham Hough, *Image and Experience*, pp. 36-42.

If, critically speaking, a major element of Eliot's "modernism" was a modern view of the past, and a readiness to make use of it, his poetry was modern in more direct ways. In the simple matter of décor, Eliot was by no means the first man to put in verse the urban nightmare with its fragmented or submerged or stencilled sub-characters; but he saw it and saw through it, relating it across time and space to other patterns, congruent shapes, saw it as a novelty and a repetition, both. And he made use of devices for constructing this vision that no one in English had ever used with anything like his complexity and assurance. These are perfectly exterior and elementary observations, and they ignore altogether the vexed question of who did what to the manuscript of *The Waste Land*. But, taking that poem as an individual achievement (which for fifty years it was), they do a good deal to account for its authority as the prototypical "modern" poem. And if we select a line like "O O O O that Shakespeherian rag," we can see that the modern décor (jazz rhythm) has in fact provided Eliot with a bold, brash way of saying something in brief compass about a complicated state of consciousness, in which the present contemplates the past.[8] In a different yet analogous way, I think something wonderful is done to Goldsmith's line by simply putting another syllable on it: "When lovely woman stoops to folly and . . ." An off-

---

[8] It is not the content of the line, or its implications, or its tone, even; it is the very fact that Eliot felt free to incorporate it, as an *objet trouvé*, in his poem, that gives the line its contemporary sense. Pound appreciated it, and for the same reason that he contributed the immense expression "got demobbed" to *The Waste Land*. It was a phrase beyond Eliot's power to discover or create, beyond the power of any of his translators (Signor Praz, Professor Curtius, or Jean de Menasce) to render.

rhythm like this, or a trick of syncopation as in the previous example, involves the modern, not as mere passive subject-matter, but as an active energy, one strong voice in a diphthong defined precisely at both ends, in time.

The central cluster of images around which *The Waste Land* organizes one deep layer of feeling is provided by the intertwined themes of sex, love, and primitive ritual. I do not have anything to add to what has long been recognized here, except to emphasize the clinical tone in which the demonstration is conducted, its dry, Flaubertian exactness. Pathos is as inappropriate as romantic amplitude: putting a record on the gramophone is a gesture of despair as ultimate as expiatory suicide used to be. Love is a phantom and sex a nervous habit; only the fouled underground stream of primitive feeling still flows in the buried mind of the city as through its sewers. It is the sense of utter personal contamination that Eliot has caught in this net of sexual metaphor—and a metaphor is what sex amounts to in *The Waste Land*, a vehicle for alien and impersonal purposes. In his sense of this deep invasion, and of the absolute barrenness of the "freedom" that frames it, Eliot was not of course permanently or distinctively modern. A theme as broad as sexual disgust is not the private property of any age. But Frazer and Freud, in serving the same purpose for Eliot as Leo Africanus and his astral cronies served for Yeats, brought into his poetry not only a way of making sex summarize the anxieties of a civilization, but a way of seeing so-called high culture against the background of the primitive, as its jailer and perhaps executioner. It was, it remains, a major modern theme. Eliot was aided in giving it the proper dry, hard expression by a stream of clinical, or quasi-scientific images, remote, impersonal, taxonomic:

137

Princess Volupine's phthisic hand, the fractured atoms of Gerontion, and others that will come to mind.[9]

And I confess—though this is only a passing observation, and I should have learned from long experience that one does not triumph over Professor deMan with an off-hand observation—that it is an explicit recognition of these active technical resources of the modern, these anthropological tatters, syncopated rhythms, pedantic terminologies, and wry clusters of contaminated attitudes gathered into one sharp discord—that seems to me most distressingly missing from his account of literary modernity.[10] The modern is not just a problem; it includes an answer, or set of answers, or materials for a literary answer, as a modern musician can count on ears tuned to hear discords that one hundred years ago would have been mere agony. Eliot at least never overlooked these prehensile, active energies of the modern, nor their ability to make the familiar different, the past past and the present a special way of looking at it. Eliot's remark to the man who complained that the classic authors were remote from us "because we know so much more than they do" is an old chestnut by now, but it embodies a useful three-quarter truth. "Precisely," he said, "and they are that which we know." The addition to be made is that the way we know them is who we are, or a good way of defining us.

Two kinds of imagery, differing from one another yet somehow felt to be compatible, and both relatively new to English verse, embodied the new vision. Old meta-

[9] I am indebted to my colleague John Espey for pointing out this streak of Laforguian imagery in Eliot's poems through the 1920's—and the almost complete absence of anything equivalent in the later poetry.

[10] "Literary History and Literary Modernity," in *Blindness and Insight* (Oxford University Press, 1971), p. 142.

phors may describe them, but they need to be defined a bit more narrowly than is usual. The hard-surface image, presenting the object as a vivid, clean-cut, sensual experience, is associated, in English literature at least, with Imagism; the translucent image, read subsurface through its overtones and reverberations, ties into the category of Symbolism. Recent commentators like Donald Davie have emphasized the contrast between the two styles, their incompatibility;[11] this is right, but not one hundred percent right. On certain levels they do go together. First negatively, in cutting off a horizontal decorative flow from image to image, in abrogating the familiar alliance of description and moral reflection. And then positively, in forcing the reader to construct the significant shape of the poem multi-directionally, out of a set of given points, into a constellation built out of the relations and distances between its different images. In all this the two "schools" are alike; the difference is simply that one (Symbolism) admits if it does not actively make subterranean connections by means of implication and overtone, while the other (Imagism) offers merely a vacancy, an absence of overt relatedness. In an early review Eliot speaks of American poets as particularly "fearful of betraying any reaction beyond that revealed in the choice and arrangement. . . . The Russian influence [he continues] may here count for something; the Russian novel with its curious trick of fastening upon accidental properties of a critical situation and letting them in turn fasten upon the attention to such an extent as to replace the emotion which gave them their importance."[12] By "the Russian novel," Eliot in this passage pretty clearly means Dostoevsky; but the technical

[11] "Pound and Eliot" in *Eliot in Perspective*, ed. Graham Martin (New York, 1970), pp. 62-82.
[12] "Reflections on Contemporary Poetry," *Egoist*, IV, 8 (September 1917), pp. 118-19.

trick he describes, with its interchange of emotion and object, could be reconciled without much difficulty to a description of an Imagist poem, a Symbolist poem, or a poem making use of an "objective correlative." Only the meaning of the word "accidental" needs clarification in the light of the two exceptions, "choice" and "arrangement." I think Eliot elected the word "accidental" to express distance, independence of literal assertion, and a relationship created by the reader as well as found in the structure of things by the writer.[13] His own predilection—though reservations can still be heard echoing in the passage—was evidently for a loosely controlled translucent, rather than an opaque, use of language.

Linguistic translucency, loose almost to the point of indeterminacy, was another of those simple technical innovations the implications of which took a number of years to explore. When words are used in the normal discursive way with a single referent—"this book," "this desk"—the word, though translucent, is a univocal, that is, a strictly limited, sign of its object. But words may be translucent to many other things too—translucent to their own etymologies and analogues, translucent to the attitude of a speaker expressed or implied, translucent to the secondary meanings of different contexts, translucent to their relation with other words, and to the ways other people have used this particular word. Whether language can ever be absolutely opaque, barring resolute nonsense on the part of the writer and deliberate insensitivity on the part of the reader, may be debated; but absolute

[13] There is, of course, a technical philosophical meaning to the word, as well, that may not have been absent from Eliot's mind: but the distinction between accident and being is Aristotelian, not Bradleyan. The kind of recurrent phrase or image that sticks in Raskolnikov's mind when he is trying not to think of something is probably what Eliot has in mind as an "accidental property."

opacity and complete translucence (which are almost convertible terms) do not in either case leave us with much to say about language in relation to anything else. The more frequent procedure is for literary language to be or seem relatively opaque in one sector in order to direct the reader's insight toward another. Just as in post-Impressionist painting, when the referents cannot possibly be assembled in the represented order (in the natural world there cannot be as many immense cocks poised in the sky as Chagall sees there), we assemble them in another order—visionary, decorative, expressive, symbolic, whatever. So when Prufrock tells us he

> should have been a pair of ragged claws
> Scuttling across the floors of silent seas,

the language opens a space for us to fill with half a dozen or so middle terms, at our option.

In one sense, language that is thoroughly de-*thing*ified, and therefore only about its own processes (as in Valéry) is really translucent *and* opaque; there is no use to look for or arrange the referents; all we need do is respond to the ideal order that is the pure poem, the dance of images as things in their own right. It is in this sense and at this level that the Imagist poem and the Symbolist poem clasp hands. And it is this sort of poem that *The Waste Land* (though it makes use of both Imagist and Symbolist techniques) is not, was not, and did not aspire to be. The center of consciousness is never scrutinized directly; the poem never confronts its own vision or mode of language; for better or worse, it is a social poem, about things out there. It sees "modern" experience and, not without resistance, sees through it, but to a very dubious and problematic ultimate, to very little that can be felt as opaque. That may make the poem look as if the "subject matter"

141

were still caged in a futile idealist framework—as indeed I think it is. Its major theme, as I see it, is the lack of that rooted philosophy of man that Mr. Hough blames Eliot and Pound for not creating or finding at the heart of the modernist movement. This failure of philosophy does not have much to do with the binds, however painful, involved in Bradley's theories of cognition—it has rather to do with the war and its consequences. Before a poet of 1920 could be a man talking to his fellowmen, his first question was bound to be whether they actually existed as human beings, or had any prospect of doing so, and if not, why not? In a famous essay written specifically for translation and publication in the *Atheneum* (April and May 1919), Valéry characterized "La crise de l'ésprit" as the moment when Europe shivered to its marrowbones at the imminence of mass suicide, total barbarism. There was, as Valéry described it, a moment of blind trauma:

"Then, as if in a desperate defence of its physiological being and possessions, the entire memory of Europe returned, in disorder. Its great men, its great books, rose up pell-mell. . . . And in the same state of mental disorder, in response to the same sense of anguish, cultured Europe experienced the sudden return to life of all its innumerable thoughts, dogmas, philosophies, heterogeneous ideals; the three hundred fashions of explaining the world, the thousand and one nuances of Christianity, the two dozen versions of positivism; the whole ghostly spectrum (spectre) of the intellectual light spread forth its incompatible color-schemes, casting a fitful glow on the agony of the European soul. [While mechanical inventors were trying to find ways of neutralizing barbed wire, catching submarines, or shooting down planes], the soul of Europe invoked, as a bloc, all the incantations known to it, recalled for serious consideration all its strangest prophecies; it sought for refuges, clues, consolations in the entire register of memories, buried actions, ancestral attitudes. And these are the known consequences of anxiety, the disordered undertakings of the brain reeling from reality to nightmare and back from nightmare to reality, as frantic as a rat in a trap. . . ."

Such was the moment of *The Waste Land*—a moment of panic before a void, of grappling up all the familiar fetishes in the hope of finding one that would stand solid against that vacancy; and such I think were some of the ingredients making for its modernity. If it was a modernity of linguistic technique alone, that fact was itself rooted in a contemporary circumstance. To forget that specific context is, I think, to risk overlooking the modernity of Eliot's poem entirely—to be misled as I think Professor Lowry Nelson is misled when he describes Eliot's use of Baudelaire's line,

—Hypocrite lecteur,—mon semblable,—mon frère!

as an Arnoldian touchstone.[14] The incongruity seems to me absolute: on the one hand, Arnold's critic, judiciously discriminating the distinguished from the mediocre by the application of a secure yardstick; on the other, Eliot's haunted encounter with a man known only by the name of his bowler and the abrupt recall of complicity in guilt. Seen in context, the line serves Eliot in no way as a criterion of judgment, but rather as what Valéry says it might be, a refuge, a clue, a consolation. (We recall that the first French translation of *The Waste Land*, which Eliot supervised, bore the title, "La terre mise à nu.")

In the measure that a poem commits itself to the "mo-

[14] "The Fictive Reader and Literary Self-Reflexiveness" in *The Disciplines of Criticism*, ed. Demetz, Greene, and Nelson (Yale University Press, 1968), p. 177.

dernity" of its special moment, it becomes dependent on historical imagination in later readers. We do not have much trouble adapting to this circumstance when we read "Absalom and Achitophel"; for some reason it seems to be harder when a period of our own life has to be seen as historical. Professor Bateson, looking at Eliot's use of citations from earlier authors (which he still characterizes, after all these years, as "plagiarisms"), can find no reason for it other than a magpie's instinct for shining fragments of imagery or phraseology.[15] It seems like a remarkable judgment for the year 1970, but who knows? Professor Bateson may have been subtly parodying someone. At any rate, the reason my generation read Eliot avidly was that we saw him in something closer to Valéry's light than Bateson's. We thought he meant something, and meant it earnestly, almost in anguish. The ways in which he expressed it bore multiple analogies to other crises of consciousness beyond the immediate sphere of his poem, however we defined or avoided defining that. In short, we felt that Eliot had made literature out of several large areas of modern experience, including some rather painful aching voids that no one else seemed to know what to do with. I am not yet persuaded that we were deceived.

The material for making this case lies, I think, primarily in "Prufrock," *The Waste Land*, and a few closely associated poems. The satiric quatrain poems and *The Hollow Men*, interesting as they are in different ways, lie outside the area of my essential claim. To be sure, "Sweeney Agonistes" is one direction in which the satires point, and that splintered branch of a fascinating experiment seems (as we can now see with the benefit of *The*

[15] "The Poetry of Learning," in *Eliot in Perspective*, ed. Graham Martin, p. 39.

Waste Land manuscript) to be itself tangential and contributory—like "Gerontion"—to the vision of the big poem. But I do not think we are wrong in seeing "Prufrock" and *The Waste Land* as the central documents of Eliot's modernism, such as it was; I think the two poems can even be related developmentally without forcing analogy into too arch a contortion. "Prufrock" is the dramatic monologue of a quasi-person in a disintegrating state; the epyllion is a dramatic monologue of postwar, disintegrated Europe, expressed through a set of quasi-persons.

On this view, the moment of *The Waste Land* was for Eliot a moment of convergence and crisis—personal, intellectual, stylistic, and cultural. For an instant he held the principles of lost or potential order and actual disorder in balanced, violent antipathy within his mind. This was the moment too in the poet's technical development when he was free to draw on both Symbolist and Imagist techniques, welding them into bold dramatic lines rooted in Jacobean tragedy, and holding them under that degree of loose control which made his work so widely suggestive. He was imbued with a sense of discordant gestural rhythm, partly intuitive, partly derived from recent music, ballet, and cinema (Stravinsky and Massine); and he had newly looked into the great primitive phantasmagoria revealed by the Cambridge school of anthropologists—a vision that has deeply tinctured the whole modern conception of culture.[16] All this furniture he put,

[16] *The Golden Bough* had been flowering, volume by volume, between 1890 and 1915; in addition, Frazer's edition of Apollodorus, which appeared for the Loeb Classical Library in 1921, contained explicit and suggestive notes on the Tiresias story (I, 360-67). There is an irony in the fact that Pound seems to have contributed the deeper tone to *The Waste Land*, while Eliot (generally considered a more "serious" man) apparently thought he

deliberately or otherwise, into a house that was a little too big for it—that left room (if only because Pound's reverberant syncretism did not bed down easily with Eliot's episodic satire) for shock, surprise, uncertainty.

How brief and distinctive this period was in Eliot's career we can appreciate by glancing momentarily at *Four Quartets*. I am not comparing the merits and demerits of the late and the early poetry—though I will register a passing personal conviction that the *Quartets* rise higher in lyric intensity and sink lower toward the patter of bemused discourse than the earlier poems. (I feel J. W. Dunne and the Council for the Defence of Church Principles as close behind the one as Valéry and Stravinsky were behind the other.) On another level altogether, the technique of the *Quartets* is in good part discursive and Wordsworthian; the musical organization involving mainly repetition and thematic variation, the poems can be seen as a set of meditations departing from landscapes. With their lyrical moments and alternating streaks of flat, discursive comment, these meditations render most expressively that rhythm of vital commitment and recurrent sterility or vacancy which inevitably marks devotion to an unchanging ideal. But the world they take for granted is one that neither George Herbert nor John Keble would find strange; and what jars on this world is dismissed with an assurance about the availability of exemption from the common lot that the modern temper does not easily concede. Again and again the poet of the *Quartets* puts himself in a privileged position, passing as-

had written a funny satiric poem in the vein cultivated by the satiric poems of the 1920 volume. One important ingredient here is *pace*; Pound had a much stronger sense than Eliot of the rapidity of modern life and the change in modern reading habits; see his review of Cocteau's *Poésies* in *The Dial*, June 1921, p. 110.

sured judgment, for instance, on the vacancy of lives built on the concept of development—

> a partial fallacy,
> Encouraged by superficial notions of evolution,
> Which becomes, in the popular mind, a means of
>   disowning the past.

This tone of languid condescension can only be embarrassing. I am not tempted to justify it (Mr. Kenner warns me against doing this) as a deliberately second-rate poem.[17] But it is only the adverb that will not hold water. Eliot's slackness rises out of a viewpoint that achieves intensity only when it can abridge and compress history into a tightly folded pattern. That pattern is defined in deliberately traditional images—rose, fire, dance, the circling seasons, the four elements. The tightness of its control when it is achieved, the slackness of the verse when it is not, contrast with the more rhetorical but more reverberant looseness of *The Waste Land*. The ebb and flow of feeling in the *Quartets*, the running ground-bass of drift and loss and half-recovery, serve to create a low devout melancholy before which the very concept of the "modern" is brash and alien. This is not by any means a matter exclusively of deepening and intensification. Behind the achievement of *Four Quartets*—an achievement

---

[17] *The Invisible Poet* (New York, 1959), p. 314. Donald Davie, evidently a bolder reader, tells me flatly that the whole of "The Dry Salvages" is a parody—thus the incompetence turns out to be a dazzling virtuosity: "T. S. Eliot: the End of an Era," in *The Twentieth Century*, CLIX, no. 950 (April 1956). The explanation points to its position among the other quartets, but does not seem consistent with the fact that Eliot originally published it as a separate poem; and of course the whole idea that a man of Eliot's beliefs would write a parody of a hymn to the Virgin shows something less than sensitivity to the attunements of his mind.

the full dimensions of which I have obviously not tried to define—I am not the first to sense a kind of shrinking from hard ideas to soft ones, from an order reached or at least sought through vision to an order standing this side of vision and substituted for it.

The aspect under which we look at Eliot's career is bound to control the shape we see in it and its relation to any conceivable modernity. Most of the models set before us so far seem to me essentially linear, though the lines they pursue are rather different. Mr. Kenner, for example, describes an Eliot who remains consistently close to the principles of Bradley's skeptical, idealist metaphysics— an elusive, corrosive, disembodied intelligence lurking behind various masks and facades, including finally that of a cultural elder statesman. An inherent problem with this view is, obviously, the matter of explaining how a man who sees all minds as uncommunicating and essentially isolated finite centers can lay major emphasis on literary and cultural tradition. It is not easy to see what sort of tradition can exist for minds caught in the Bradleyan cage. Even in handling Eliot's own work, Kenner tends to dismiss large areas of it as mere camouflage or parody, protective coloration or deliberate neutrality—a surface distraction behind which a remote intelligence goes about its linguistic work, in something very close to privacy.

Equally linear, but scarcely congruent in any detail with Kenner, is the outline of Eliot's career sketched in the fourth chapter of *Poets of Reality* by Hillis Miller. Indeed, Eliot began his development, Miller agrees, in Bradley's logical box; "Prufrock" exemplifies it—the speaker is isolated in his own arbitrary definitions of space and time,

148

enclosed in the bubble of his own consciousness.[18] But, starting with *The Waste Land* or shortly thereafter, the poet starts to achieve a fleeting communication and a shared order, based primarily on emotion. The transition here is very ambiguous and undefined; when Miller starts talking about Eliot's creation of order, it is by no means clear whether the order suddenly appeared in some particular poem or was immanent in all of them all along, whether it grew out of a new experience or out of a new way of seeing old experiences. In any event, Mr. Miller shortly declares that Eliot, some time after *The Waste Land*, shattered the opaque sphere of the Bradleyan self, and found himself surrounded by real space, genuine time, and the authenticating presence of God. In the new monism that this discovery made possible, the problem of communication between self and self was solved, along with the problem of order and disorder, and most other problems. Instead of soliloquy, or painful self-expression through discovered or created objective correlatives, the poet now need only put himself in the presence of a collective and divinely infused mind. He is himself a catalyst at most, in whose presence the tradition extends itself, rearranges its counters, finds its voice. The escape from idealism, with its threat of ultimate solipsism, has been found through the Incarnation.

Miller's account is not exempt, any more than Kenner's, from internal difficulties. The transitions from stage to stage are edgy things, and very little documented in the poet's own declarations—for such important transitions, they take place in very allusive and peripheral ways, almost in paraphrase. Their chronology is also a bit blurry. The first signs of the change are signalled for Miller by

[18] *Poets of Reality* (Harvard, 1965), p. 149.

149

"Tradition and the Individual Talent," which was written and published (1919) in the middle of the most ironic and disintegrative stage of Eliot's work. And, finally, the consequences of the new attitude, as declared by Miller, have been far from apparent, even to those who have had them pointed out. *"Four Quartets,"* Mr. Graham Martin says flatly, "offers nothing so confident as an affirmation of the human body and the world's body."[19] Of course he is right. The circling dance of "East Coker," which signifies matrimony, blurs into the subway riders on the circle line who are emblems of vacancy and meaninglessness. At most the *Quartets* offer an effort at affirmation, a weak two cheers for Incarnation. The one thing they do not convey is a sacramental view of the world, a rich dwelling in the holy joy of ordinary things. The plays are even more explicit. It is with real contempt that Harry Monchensey turns Wishwood over to his stupid brother John; it is a moral caste system that appoints Celia Coplestone to martyrdom and condemns the Chamberlaynes to the drudgery of a self-assigned mediocrity.

But if Eliot neither dwelt contentedly in the house of Bradley, nor escaped from it very convincingly, in what terms shall we represent his career? Between the terms as given, a compromise is not very hard to work out. As a matter of intellectual principles, Miller may well be right; Eliot's religious conversion was a conversion away from the sterile, skeptical isolation of Bradleyan philosophy. But Eliot never worked out the stylistic or human implications of that Incarnation to which he evidently attached such importance. It always remained for him (as it is very likely to remain for Puritans—compare, for example, Milton's "Nativity Ode" with Crashaw's "In the Holy

[19] *Eliot in Perspective*, p. 130, in allusion to *Poets of Reality*, p. 185.

Nativity"), a bright light, an abstraction, a principle. Paradoxically enough, he had difficulty finding an objective correlative for Incarnation—indeed, he may have turned to Incarnation precisely because it offered to do for him what he could not do for himself. In the matter of tonal perception, on the other hand, my impulse is to side with Mr. Kenner. I think Eliot continued to lurk rather ironically, elusively, impersonally, as the completely Invisible Poet, behind even the "intermittently Christian"[20] tonality of the *Quartets*. He was not as invisible as Kenner's book deliberately makes him appear, but the habit of his mind involved irresistible reservations, and any sort of incarnation is a terrible commitment.

But under larger aspects, I would propose that a linear view of Eliot simply will not work, whatever the straight-edge we use. Indeed, he was not a modernist poet except briefly and in a limited sense when the path of his development intersected, in the platinum presence of Pound, with that of the general consciousness; more importantly, he was not given to developing in consecutive patterns at all. The pattern of a fold or turn in the direction of his thought has already made itself evident in the doctrine of tradition, where a step toward the new can be taken only by revaluating an immense number of steps already taken (an immediate obverse of this thought is that revaluation of the past relates intimately to concerns of the present and the future). In matters of religion, it was skepticism pushed to its absolute limits that became the unshakable foundation of his faith (like Dryden's); and we have seen him turning, in his chosen poetic structures, from models like Mallarmé and Valéry to models like Wordsworth and Arnold. Even in imagery we see him moving from the radical, the discordant, and the provocatory to the dec-

[20] *The Invisible Poet,* p. 306.

orative and even the deliberately archaic—that image of the dance which so entranced Professor Miller. Mr. Wollheim, speaking of the turn away from Bradley, which he has documented thoroughly, gives the move a preliminary dimension when he says that "Eliot, in the pursuit of a certain kind of security or reassurance that we are in no position to define, was progressively led to substitute, in his mind, on the one hand, ideas of less content for ideas of more content, and, on the other hand, poorer or softer ideas for better or stronger ideas." That seems partly right; but the ideas also existed sometimes, not successively, but side by side in his mind in the mixture of profound and superficial that Bernard Bergonzi finds in *Notes Toward a Definition of Culture*.[21] In addition, I am not convinced that Eliot's astringent and reactive ideas were either placatory or security-oriented. Certainly, in many of the milieux he frequented, royalism, Anglo-Catholicism, and the rest (including Maurras' brand of Catholic action) were more like red rags than white flags.

No, Eliot's lifelong habit of turning back from his own habit of thought resists facile explanation. The dialectic of skepticism, its easy conversion to fideism and royalism, we know. But fideism and royalism are rather special experiences when one has only the vestige of a church and an apology for a status quo to repose upon. One takes, then, to the second-rate or the makeshift, not for security's sake (there is no security), but on Hobson's principle: it is that or nothing. Such thinking generally leaves behind any commitment growing out of it a ghostly mental reservation or two, a twinge of leftover, undisposable awareness. That malaise, that dis-ease, is not an unalloyed distinction, a triumph of agile ingenuity (as

21 Wollheim, "Eliot and F. H. Bradley," in *Eliot in Perspective*, p. 190; Bergonzi, *T. S. Eliot* (New York, 1972), pp. 156-62.

Mr. Kenner would have it); neither is it a weakness to be overcome by an act of will or choice (as Mr. Miller proposes). It is an ambiguous intimacy, an entangled revulsion. In literary structure it implies—both as triumphant cause and pathetic effect—a turning away from the Renaissance principles of *copia* and *plenum* to the modern principles of vacancy and implosion. Now that the substantial *topoi* on which Eliot made his reputation as a "modern" poet are becoming part of history's jerky slide-show, it may be that this lurking sense of not quite belonging, not quite fitting, of having put on ill-fitting, second-rate ideas like an ill-fitting, second-rate world, will be part of Eliot's claim to the semi-permanent modernity of a classic.

Michael Goldman

FEAR IN THE WAY: THE DESIGN OF ELIOT'S DRAMA

"NOTHING is more dramatic than a ghost," says Eliot,[1] and his remark offers an illuminating technical insight into every play he wrote. It also has the virtue of forcing us to think specifically about drama, rather than, say, prosody or moral philosophy. Eliot's own practice as a critic and reputation as a poet have tended to concentrate discussion on either the versification and language of his plays or their Christian implications, and this, while leading to much excellent and valuable criticism, has helped promote a serious misunderstanding of his achievement as a dramatist—as a writer, that is, whose texts are designed to allow a group of actors to shape an audience's experience in a theater over a finite interval of time. The possum-like tone Eliot reverts to in discussing most aspects of his dramaturgy other than verse and idiom has encouraged the notion that in matters of dramatic design, particularly the shaping of the action and the use of dra-

[1] *Selected Essays*, 3rd ed. (London, 1951), p. 52.

155

matic convention, Eliot was content to follow the techniques of the commercial theater, and not always the most up-to-date techniques at that. The picture that emerges seems to be of an Eliot laboring to do indifferently what Noel Coward did well, in the hope that verse meditations on the Christian life might somehow be smuggled to an audience while it was being diverted by boulevard entertainment. But if we allow Eliot the benefit of the doubt and approach his plays as the work of a serious dramatist, we can form quite a different impression of their design and of the originality and value of their achievement.

So I turn to the matter of ghosts in order to stress Eliot's art as a dramatist. Attention to the dramatic value of ghosts in his plays will help us see how they are constructed, what precise use they make of the conventions of drawing-room comedy, and why Eliot's achievement in the theater runs considerably deeper than the creation of a mode of dramatic verse.

Drama probably began with ghosts, with prehistoric impersonations intended to transfigure the malice of spirits—to indulge, placate, or wrestle with the dead, to turn Furies into Eumenides. Ghosts are dramatic because they make for action. By their very nature they stimulate that flow of aggression on which all drama depends. Ghosts haunt us—that is, they bring aggression to bear on us in an especially volatile way, a way that penetrates with particular intensity to our psyche and encourages imitation, encourages us to haunt as we are haunted. They are hard to defend against; they cannot easily be subdued or ignored. They create an unstable situation in the external world because their victims must transfer their aggression to new objects. When a real person hits us we can either hit him back or refuse to. Either reaction may make for drama, but the exchange can easily be enclosed, a balance quickly restored. We cannot hit back at a ghost, however, any more than we can ignore him. The haunting transmits itself through us to a wider world. Thus the classical device of a ghost crying for revenge precipitates the great Elizabethan discoveries as to plot and action—perhaps the greatest discovery being that the ghost could be internalized in the figure of the revenger, who could then be a fully human character—and starring part—while retaining a ghost's peculiar interest and privileges. The ghost makes easy and intense a kind of psychic thrust and counterthrust that connects inner states of feeling—desire, fear, hatred—with movement and change in the external world, the transformation, essential to drama, of activity into action.

A theory of ghosts might make a good theory of drama, and the historical version of this theory might note that at about the point in time when audiences cease to believe in ghosts they begin to be haunted by memories. People have always had memories, of course, but I would suggest that they are not *haunted* by memories much before Rousseau. In any historical period drama must find its proper ghosts, sources for haunting that an audience can accept as both meaningful and mysterious. Today, for example, we are haunted by unconscious memories as well as conscious ones, and by the past in the form of our parents, our bodies, our economic and social milieu. These are the ghosts that walk the modern stage, many of them, perhaps all, first set walking there by Ibsen.

I sketch this theory of the ghost both to suggest how richly sensitive to the art of the drama Eliot's remark is, and also by way of providing a background for his own ghosts and what he does with them. The structure of each of Eliot's plays is built on a double manifestation of ghosts. At first, the play appears to be haunted by spirits that, though in some respects disconcertingly archaic, still bear a clear relation to our own familiar ghosts—the ghosts we have been accustomed since Ibsen to recognize both in drama and in our lives. Gradually—and this is the fundamental process of Eliot's drama—the ghosts are revealed to be very different from what we took them to be. The original ghosts seem to vanish with an ease that is again disconcerting, but their vanishing proves to be a deeper haunting, more personally directed at the audience. They have turned into other, more persistent, ghosts. The most intense and usually the most effective part of Eliot's drama is not the demonstration that the new ghosts are different, but the manifestation of their true power to haunt—their power to haunt in their true capacity.

Eliot gives his spirits many names. But whether he simply calls them ghosts, as in *The Elder Statesman*, or shadows, furies, spectres, phantoms, spooks, guardians, or even saints and martyrs, it is as ghosts that they perform dramatically. They haunt the characters and inspire the action. Like the Furies in *The Family Reunion* they are often quite explicitly associated with myth or legend, but they also conform to ideas a modern audience can accept. They are ghosts of past associations and deeds, of heredity and environment. The guardians in *The Cocktail Party* may seem enigmatic when considered as guardians of souls, but Reilly is quite familiar to us in his professional role as a guardian of psyches. The ghosts are all versions of the "fear in the way"—the phrase from Ecclesiastes that Eliot used as a working title for *Murder in the Cathedral*[2]—a fear that turns out to be both rele-

[2] See E. Martin Browne, *The Making of T. S. Eliot's Plays* (Cambridge, 1969), pp. 54-55.

vant and irrelevant to the concerns of the characters, and that must be met in the course of the action and either accepted or put aside. In fact, the fear in the way of each play is first to be put aside and then accepted. At the end of each play the false ghosts have disappeared and the true ghosts hover with their horror, boredom, and glory over the characters.

Let me very briefly illustrate this by tracing the pattern for each of the plays in turn, from *Murder in the Cathedral* to *The Elder Statesman*. In *Murder in the Cathedral*, the shadows with which Thomas must struggle appear at first to be the Tempters, ghosts of former desires whose enticements to do the wrong thing are quickly dismissed, leaving Thomas to face his real struggle with the temptation to do the right thing for the wrong reason. At the same time there is another spirit in the play haunting the women of Canterbury. It is a fear of Thomas in his capacity as saint and martyr, fear of his coming to Canterbury and of the act of martyrdom to which they are compelled to bear witness. The action of the play demonstrates that this fear is illusory. In one sense the play shows the women are wrong to feel haunted, but in another sense—to which the Knights and the final chorus direct us—the burden of fear and anguish attaching to the figure of St. Thomas remains with them and with us at the end of the play and is indeed revealed only by the play's complete action.

In *The Family Reunion* the pattern is less effectively worked out, but it is simple and clear. The Furies of course begin as Harry's apparent guilt in the death of his wife, the source of his self-loathing and loathing for the human condition. In facing up to them under this aspect, he learns that while their meaning is illusory, they are nevertheless real. They are in fact "bright angels," his

Eumenides, whom he must follow. We are left, as in *Murder in the Cathedral*, with a distinctly earthbound chorus burdened by fear and a sense of isolation.

The guardians of *The Cocktail Party* are menacing in a manner that conforms to the prevailing tone of high comedy—they harass Edward with embarrassing questions and surprise visits, they press loathsome concoctions and cryptic advice upon him. It is enough, by Edward's own admission—and this is a point that must be seized in playing—to humiliate him. Their power to humiliate depends of course on the memories and miseries of his relation to Lavinia. Lavinia is described at one point as a phantom; she, brought back from the dead, also haunts Edward as he haunts her. The guardians turn out not to be pests, but, once more, bright angels, yet their power to haunt persists. Most of the complaints Edward and Lavinia bring against each other are disposed of, but their central misery is not. It is Celia who escapes the emptiness and isolation of the ordinary lot, and Edward and Lavinia are left facing both her terrifying example and the absence of transcendent love in their own lives. The mood is hopeful, for their acceptance is a genuine spiritual accomplishment, but a variety of ghosts, of whom Celia must be counted one, haunt the ordinary people who are left behind.

The characters in *The Confidential Clerk* are haunted by disappointments, ghosts of absence—missing children and parents, lost sources of vocation and relatedness. There are also guardian-like figures, Mrs. Guzzard and Eggerson (though lost children haunt them too), whose riddling style imparts a kind of harassment to the persistent memory of these absent spirits, a method similar to that of the guardians in *The Cocktail Party*, who play teasingly upon what is haunting in Edward's and Lavinia's lives. The missing children and parents function as negative bright angels. Their absence seems to leave Sir Claude and Lady Mulhammer, Lucasta Angel, B. Kaghan, and even Colby lacking a meaningful connection with reality. All the missing links are restored in the last act, where Mrs. Guzzard dominates, but the restored relations are in the end far from Eumenidean, except in the case of Colby. The play's focus narrows to Sir Claude, as Colby slips out with Mrs. Guzzard. Mulhammer, shaken and bewildered, is left with Lucasta, whom he has in effect ignored for most of the play. This is his real daughter and he must accept her, as well as accepting all that he does not have. Again we are left with off-stage transcendence and an ordinary figure on-stage facing the loss and insufficiency of ordinary life.

In *The Elder Statesman*, Lord Claverton tells us that Gomez and Mrs. Carghill are ghosts—ghosts of his past, of past crimes. In all the senses announced at the beginning of the play, their power to haunt Claverton turns out to be illusory; the crimes are not real crimes; their threats are insubstantial. But in another sense the ghosts and what they represent are inexpungeable; to face them they must be accepted, for their power to haunt lies in their reflection of the facts of Claverton's own character, which he must accept if he is to cease to be "hollow." For once, the burden is eased for those left on stage. Monica and Charles are brought closer to each other and to Claverton because his confrontation and acceptance of the ghosts has issued in a transforming love. But the discovery, a version of which has been hinted at in the final tableau of *The Confidential Clerk*, depends on clear-eyed acceptance of a haunting loss and limitation.

The great point about the encounter at the end of *The Elder Statesman*, and the great dramatic surprise, is that

161

Claverton does not make his ghosts disappear or render them innocuous by facing them. They continue to be what they always were, and their power for evil is all the more felt for being more fully faced. The price Claverton pays is his son, Michael, but the meaning of the price, as he tells us, is love. If *The Elder Statesman* goes beyond *The Confidential Clerk* by presenting human love as a path to Divine Love, it is significant that the parent-child relation it requires as a dramatic pivot is much grimmer than that between Sir Claude and his daughter. Lucasta is quite clearly a bright angel, as her name suggests. Michael Claverton is not, and he follows Gomez and Carghill.

The pattern I have been describing is suggestive in a number of ways as to the meaning and method of Eliot's drama. What I wish to stress now is its relation to the convention he finally chose to work in—the convention of boulevard entertainment whose fourth-wall realism and bourgeois milieu sustain the workings of a well-made plot. The exact genre may vary with the mood required, but it is always well-made, whether it be the plot of detection, love-intrigue, farce, or melodrama—always the mechanism of secrets to be discovered, obstacles to be overcome, communications to be rechanneled and restored. It will already be clear that the transition from false ghost to true ghost corresponds to the development in every one of Eliot's plays by which the expectations of the convention are subverted. *The Family Reunion* is not an Agatha Christie-like story of crime and punishment but of sin and expiation. The love-tangles of Edward and Celia, Lavinia and Peter, do not lead to complications in the second and third act. Mrs. Guzzard's revelations do not solve the problems carefully established in the first two acts of *The Confidential Clerk*, but show that the

162

problem as it has been stated is irrelevant, and so on. More important, the change in our understanding of the ghosts develops its special meaning and intensity only by virtue of taking place in this type of setting and growing out of this type of dramatic convention.

The well-made play, particularly the drawing-room comedy or mystery, is characterized by an emphasis on mechanical connectedness. The introduction of any significant element implies that this element will be seen to mesh like a gear with all the other elements of the play, and the action of the play will be the operation of all these gears like a single machine. If the key to a letterbox is called attention to in the first act, a significant letter must be unlocked in the last. This sense of mechanical connectedness extends to the society of the play. The characters' lives, pasts, and appetites act upon each other to a degree of intimacy and efficiency that may fairly be taken, in this genre, as an index of the play's success. The result is not always mechanical drama in any pejorative sense, and the connections I am talking about are not always mechanical in the sense that they are superficial or merely physical. But the impression of efficient and causal interconnection prevails, just as it prevails in the various notions of significant action, of cause and effect—of psychological, biological, social, and economic determinism—that drama of this type reflects.

The haunted characters in Eliot's drawing-room plays are pursued by phantoms of connectedness—actions committed in the past, family secrets, old associations, lovers—the social, sexual, and psychological determinants that are the ghosts of modern drama. But in the end these baleful connections are revealed to be illusory, and the characters are seen to be truly haunted by an inability to connect. The crowded drawing room,

the carefully prepared meeting of principals, the states-
man's diary are all empty—a cheat and a disappointment.
The exact quality of this emptiness is frequently and care-
fully described—the sudden solitude in a crowded desert,
the exacerbated isolation in the midst of an apparent con-
nectedness. It is an isolation that appears inevitable and
also miserably unreal because connectedness is felt as the
only reality. And here we find the significance of Eliot's
convention. This type of isolation cannot be conveyed,
for example, on the unlocalized platform of the existential
stage, the stage of *Waiting for Godot*. There, isolation
represents reality; one is trapped and isolated *in* the real
world, the world of one's aloneness, a setting in which
the individual, terrified and despairing as he may be, can
yet be seen to possess his being. But the sense of isolation
from which Eliot's characters suffer—it strikingly resem-
bles that of schizophrenics[3]—is an isolation in unreality.

[3] Laing's account of schizophrenia in *The Divided Self* (Lon-
don, 1960) makes very interesting reading for the student of
Eliot's work. The schizophrenic, we learn, is convinced he has no
identity, that he is "hollow" and "unreal." The real world terrifies
him, afflicts him with fears of drowning and petrifaction, because
it threatens to swamp his identity, to fill up the vacuum of the
self. At the same time, because he is unreal, he can take no real
pleasure in the world; it seems to him ghostly or barren. Laing
reports the following typical dreams of a schizophrenic patient:
"I found myself in a village. I realize it has been deserted: it
is in ruins; there is no life in it. . . ."
". . . I was standing in the middle of a barren landscape. It was
absolutely flat. There was no life in sight. The grass was hardly
growing. My feet were stuck in mud. . . ."
". . . I was in a lonely place of rocks and sand. I had fled there
from something; now I was trying to get back to somewhere but
didn't know which way to go . . ."
To deal with this at once unreal and terrifying wasteland, to
protect his own vulnerable hollowness, the schizoid personality
constructs "false self systems," plausible, usually docile personae
that keep the world at a distance, prevent it from encountering

They are trapped in a world of make-believe. In this condition the familiar social world itself is haunting because the very appearance of connectedness only heightens the conviction that one is incapable of connection; one is oneself not real, an empty, worthless, hollow man. The unreal city is oneself and the key confirms the prison.

The dramaturgical point, then, is this. Like the rooms that figure so prominently in *The Waste Land* and the early poems, the drawing room and the dramatic conventions associated with it have a twofold function—they

---

the "real" self. He lives forever in a world of make-believe, which only serves to plunge him into a deeper sense of isolation, fragmentation, and worthlessness. Frequently, the schizophrenic believes himself to be invisible.

The clinical point is valuable, not for any suggestions of pathology, but because it points to a source of connection between certain groups of observations and images that are frequently juxtaposed in Eliot's poetry, most notably in *The Waste Land* and the plays. Particularly, there is the connection between, on the one hand, a sense of the world as both unreal and loathsome and, on the other, a deep doubt as to one's identity and capacity to escape from the prison of the self, a petrifying terror of contact with the outside world accompanied by a depressed conviction that such contact is impossible.

Eliot's great and continuing influence on the thought of our age stems in large measure from his portrayal of a crisis in the self, reflected in every phase of modern life, which bears an obvious resemblance to the pathological state Laing has termed "ontological insecurity." Given our inadequate understanding of schizophrenia, the mysteriousness of its etiology and its distressingly high incidence, we might do well to consider whether Eliot's vision does not suggest—as, in their own way, Laing and others in the field are beginning to suggest—that schizophrenia is a spiritual as well as a mental disorder, an affliction of our culture. When Eliot observes that "something happened to the mind of England" between Donne and Tennyson, and that what happened was a divorce between thought and feeling, it is not to be assumed that this is a "projection" of some personal experience of a familiar mental disturbance, a brush of the wing of schizophrenia. But it may be an insight into its causes.

stand for a real world with which the hero is powerless to make contact, and they also stand for the "finite center"[4] of the self in whose unreality the hero is trapped and isolated. In *The Cocktail Party* the isolated cell of the poems has become a modern flat where a man cannot get a moment's privacy, but it confirms a prison still. One achievement of *The Cocktail Party* is its transposition of so much that is haunting in modern life—the horror and boredom and glory that attack and pursue the central sensibility of *The Waste Land*—into the modes of light comedy, but though any production of the play must maintain a proper lightness, it must also be careful not to slight the real pressures that even the most farcical turns of the action apply to the major characters, especially Edward. The first act is a series of humiliations for him, all the more humiliating because they are initiated by the typical raillery and contretemps of drawing-room comedy. And it is exactly this contrast between the convention and his response that allows the play to reveal with lucidity and precision the real sources of humiliation in his life.

Though the later plays are in some respects more profoundly conceived and contain concluding passages of a theatrical beauty quite unique to them, *The Cocktail Party* is still Eliot's most successful play, because in it the vivacity of the author's line-by-line response to his theatrical opportunities is at its height. We feel this most strongly in two ways—first in the interaction of the characters, and second in the use of all the elements in the mise en scène to advance the action and to intensify and

---

[4] See "Leibniz' Monads and Bradley's Finite Centres," in Eliot's *Knowledge and Experience in the Philosophy of F. H. Bradley* (New York, 1964), pp. 198-207. Cf. *The Waste Land*, ll. 411 ff. and Eliot's note on l. 411.

render more subtle our experience of it, in particular to heighten our sense that the characters are haunted. In *Poetry and Drama* Eliot complains that too many of *The Cocktail Party*'s characters stand outside the action, but of all his plays it is *The Cocktail Party* whose characters most thoroughly act upon each other in their dialogue.[5] Not surprisingly, *The Cocktail Party* has of all the drawing-room plays the most definite spine, which can be expressed in the phrase *to begin*. From the beginning of the play, when Alex is called upon to begin his story again (the story being drowned, as Julia's soon will be, in the very effort to begin it), until the end, when the bell rings and Lavinia says, "Oh I'm glad. It's begun," the characters are constantly trying to begin and to begin again. And their efforts to begin—if only to leave the room or start a conversation—elaborate the process of haunting and heighten our sense of the fragmentation and isolation of the self that Edward, Lavinia, and Celia experience.

[5] Eliot's characters seem at times to have no immediate motivation beyond making themselves clear. The notion of action in drama is notoriously difficult to define, but we may agree that action is locally felt in the line-to-line presence of a psychic thrust, an impulse within the actor pushing out against the other actors and circumstances on stage, and that the interplay of thrusts, the push and pull between actors, is what makes dialogue playable. The thrust to clarity alone is insufficient, and there are too many telltale lines of the what-do-you-mean, explain-yourself variety in the pages of Eliot's drama. Still, in all the plays except *The Family Reunion*, and particularly in *Murder in the Cathedral* and *The Cocktail Party*, the playable thrust is very much in evidence, and it regularly reveals the presence of what I call ghosts, the haunting forces and persons who humiliate and harry the major characters.

Eliot's characters do achieve a unique clarity of expression, however, and this is an important source of power and originality in the plays. See Professor Kenner's remarkably illuminating discussion of Eliot's drama in *The Invisible Poet* (New York, 1959), pp. 334-36.

167

The mise en scène contributes throughout to the sense of an illusory connectedness badgering and isolating the central characters. Take, for example, the strange variety of food that is prepared, consumed, or recommended in the opening scenes. The inadequate tidbits, Alex's culinary fantasies and inedible offerings, the remedies of Norwegian cheese, curry powder, prunes, and alcohol, even the unwanted champagne, all forced upon Edward as he suffers in his constantly interrupted yet unbreakable solitude—these like the genteel disarray of the set, the post-cocktail-party depression (and it has been a badly managed, underfed and underpopulated cocktail party)—like the set, and with a wit and variety that makes the audience alert and sympathetic to nuance, the food plays upon the isolation and debility of the untransfigured individual in the ordinary world. It is a horror and boredom expressed no less exactly than that of the poor women of Canterbury.

All this reinforces the attack Edward undergoes in the course of the first act, the series of humiliations whose insubstantial and amusing surface constantly reminds us how illusory is the ostensibly dense social continuum in which Edward has his being. He cannot be alone for a minute; everyone wants to feed him. He has no privacy; in the nicest way he is interrogated and exposed—but in truth he has nothing but his privacy, and it is a privacy that leaves him with nothing. Left to himself he "moves about restlessly," while the doorbell and the phone keep ringing. Throughout the act, Eliot emphasizes a nagging connection with the outside world by a series of exits and entrances that require Edward to half-leave the stage— to be invisible for an instant, open the door and return with his caller. Edward's world, like drawing-room comedy itself, is a network of insistent social connections

168

which, like his marriage, fail to free him from aloneness and emptiness. In the first scene, he waits his guests and interrupters out, then phones Celia only to receive no answer. The lights go down and come up again. We are immediately aware that no considerable interval has passed; the time elapsed has been pointedly insignificant. Edward sits among the debris as before—potato crisps, glasses, bottles, a forgotten umbrella—playing solitaire.[6]

These examples have all been taken from the first act. Each of the devices referred to—the emphasis on communications, the treatment of food and drink, the behavior of characters when alone—is used in later acts to underline that awareness of transformation which I have argued is essential to Eliot's dramatic technique—awareness that the true nature of the haunting in the play is being revealed. This dramatic imagery is employed with a distinctive wit, a kind of half-explicit mocking of its own recurrence and tendentiousness that sustains the play's tone. Sir Henry's office with its plot-expediting intercom and its carefully scheduled arrangement of exits and entrances contrasts nicely with the nagging persistence of bells and callers in Act One. Similarly, the toasts that are drunk in the course of the play form a sequence that guides our attention from the ordinary to the transcendent. And in the last act we have a cocktail party to contrast with that of the first. The work of the caterers and the new reputation of the Chamberlaynes' parties for good food and drink makes itself felt as a welcome improvement in this ordinary drawing-room world. Even the exits and entrances have been improved—by the presence of a caterer's man who announces the guests.

[6] Later, in the midst of their painful interview, when Celia leaves the room for a moment, "EDWARD goes over to the table and inspects his game of Patience. He moves a card."

In this world, decent social arrangements still mean much, for they are still the means by which the guardians make their presence known.

As for the behavior of the characters in private, let me take just one example—the moment when Reilly lies down on his couch. In part, this is a joke—a piece of raillery typical of the play but aimed directly at the audience. The couch is one of the indicators by which we have recognized the psychiatrist's office. It has remained empty throughout Reilly's interviews with Edward and Lavinia. Both conventional psychiatry and our conventional dramatic expectations are being mocked. This orchestrates the real shift in expectation, both for us and the characters. The problems of this marriage are not to be located in the usual psychological sources, but in an abiding spiritual deficiency. At the same time the scene marks another transition in the action and in our understanding of the characters. Reilly's moment of exhaustion precedes the entrance of Julia ("Henry, get up") and the interview with Celia; it prepares for our discovery that Reilly does not occupy the highest place in the play's spiritual hierarchy and our dawning sense of what that hierarchy may mean. Again let me stress that the spiritual world is felt as haunting, that it exerts an unsettling and mysterious psychic pressure on the characters. If Reilly's questions and Julia's snooping haunt Edward in the first act, Celia's martyrdom haunts the marital contentment of the last.

The apprehension of a source of haunting and the gradual discovery that the source is very different from what it has been apprehended to be—this pattern of action and feeling is central to Eliot's dramaturgy, and it accounts for an important feature of his dramatic style, or rather for a number of features that together enforce a single theme—that of knowing and not knowing. Take, for example, the motif of the visitor who is both expected and unexpected. The Third and Fourth Tempters both play upon this idea, but it is felt more dramatically in the later plays. Harry is known to be on his way home as *The Family Reunion* opens, but at the point of his first entrance everyone is actively expecting either Arthur or John. Harcourt-Reilly is an unexpected visitor no one is very surprised to see in either the last scene of Act One or in Act Three of *The Cocktail Party*. The arrivals of Lady Elizabeth in the first act and Mrs. Guzzard in the last act of *The Confidential Clerk*, though carefully prepared and discussed extensively in advance, are disconcerting and unexpected when they happen (and both arrivals are heralded by a series of disconcerting messengers).

Also related to the theme of knowing and not knowing is the motif of the crime that is not a crime. The old man Claverton runs over turns out in the third act to have been dead before the accident. Harry Monchensey did not murder his wife; Lucasta Angel is not Sir Claude Mulhammer's mistress; Edward has not betrayed Celia. In all cases, the revelation is casual, a throwaway defeat of our expectations; it is part of our becoming aware that certain actions and memories do not matter or do not matter for the reasons we thought they did.

Knowing-and-not-knowing is also felt in a recurrent verbal device, prominent as early as *Sweeney Agonistes*— the use of echoing dialogue. This example is from *The Cocktail Party*:

JULIA: Who is he?
EDWARD: *I* don't know.
JULIA: *You* don't know?

EDWARD: I never saw him before in my life.
JULIA: But how did he come here?
EDWARD: *I* don't know.
JULIA: *You* don't know!

As here, the cadence is usually a mocking or riddling one; we may be tempted to put it down to the Possummode of mystification. But the device turns a character's words back on himself, suggesting, as the Fourth Tempter suggests to Thomas, that a man may not know what he thinks he knows, and that we in the audience must expect some change in what we think we know. Our words may be riddles even to ourselves. In the drawing-room plays the echoing dialogue is typically both uncomprehending and disconcerting; it confirms a prison but alerts us to a key.

We know and do not know what it is to act and suffer. How do we come to know more? The answer, given in every play, is: *watch and wait*. But watching and waiting imply a crucial dramatic problem, and the success or failure of each of Eliot's plays may be said to hinge on its solution. At some point in the drawing-room plays, the dramatic convention becomes a fragmented background against which certain characters are seen in a new light, isolated in a freshly haunted world. But this means that there is a risk that the continuity of the action may evaporate, sustained as it has been by the apparent connectedness of the play's world and the now-discredited significance of the ghosts haunting it. At the same time there is the danger that the dramatic interest of the central character may evaporate too. The watching and waiting theme requires that at some moment the hero surrender his role as an agent; he must consent to be passive. He is displaced from a central initiating role to become part of the pattern. The moment of surrender may itself make for a good scene: as when Edward accepts his becoming a thing, an object in the hands of masked actors, or Mulhammer gives up control to Eggerson and Guzzard and absorbs the bewildering results. Claverton struggles with a version of this necessity in his first long speech and again accepts it in the strong scene at the end of his play, and Thomas' surrender is perhaps most powerfully felt in his long cry at the moment of death, which Eliot has considerably expanded from the historical records. But essentially what a character accepts at a moment like this is that he must no longer be a *performer*—and this has awkward implications, both for actor and playwright.

Watching and waiting over any period of time is not very dramatic; it is always a problem for an actor, and Eliot cannot be said always to have solved it. At the very end of *The Elder Statesman*, Claverton says, "In becoming no one, I begin to live," but the actor of this often ungrateful role might fairly complain that, instead of becoming no one, the play limits him to *being* no one for most of its length, that he must watch and wait from the beginning. And in *The Family Reunion*, once the interest of the false ghosts peters out and there is no crime to be uncovered, Eliot can devise no action that engages any of the characters; we are treated to a series of explanations that never become encounters. From *The Cocktail Party* on, Eliot is always able to maintain action and encounter, because the haunting function, both false and true, is taken over by real characters who can make their presence felt in a lively way whenever they appear. Reilly, Julia, Guzzard, Carghill, Gomez—these are good parts, not hard to act. But for the last two plays there remains a difficulty in casting the leading roles which makes it problematical whether *The Confidential Clerk* and *The*

Elder Statesman will ever receive performances that can test their best values. In many ways they ask more of their actors than they offer in return. Claverton must be played by an actor not only strong but abnormally unselfish, ready to pass honestly through the long passivity of the early acts in order to contribute to the lovely finale. In *The Confidential Clerk* the problem is even more serious. The characterization of Sir Claude as a financier is extremely flimsy, and his lack of definition as a public figure makes the first act dangerously slack. The deep problem, however, is Colby, whose interest lies far too much in the eyes of his beholders. He must be cast against his part; the role must be filled by an immensely engaging, physically robust actor with no suggestion of priggishness or passivity about him. Here, clearly, the production must make up for weaknesses in the text. Whether we shall ever get such a production, however, remains to be seen.

So far I have been talking mostly about the plays written after *Murder in the Cathedral*, since the subject of ghosts has a special bearing on Eliot's treatment of the drawing-room convention. But my remarks apply to the earlier play as well, for the pattern I have described helps to account for *Murder in the Cathedral*'s dramatic effectiveness and points to meanings that have been overlooked in criticism and production. Let me begin with an objection that is frequently raised against the play: "The determining flaw in *Murder in the Cathedral* is that the imitation of its action is complete at the end of Part One."[7] I do not think this is true to our felt experience of the play, even in a good amateur production, nor to the dramatic intentions clearly indicated in the text.

It is true that by the end of Part One we have seen Thomas accept his martyrdom as part of a pattern to

[7] Denis Donoghue, *The Third Voice* (Princeton, 1959), p. 81.

which he must consent for the right reasons, and that we see this acceptance re-enacted both in the sermon and in Part Two, with no modification of theme or deepening of Thomas' response. But the point of the play lies in the re-enactment, since everything is changed *for us* by each re-seeing. The aim of *Murder in the Cathedral* is to make its audience "watch and wait," to "bear witness"—to see the event in several perspectives, each enriching the other, so the pattern may subsist, so the action may be seen as pattern, and so that our own relation to the action, our part of the pattern, may be fully and intensely experienced—and this is not finally accomplished until the very end of the play.

Once more it is a question of knowing and not knowing. Even as the play begins, we know what its climax will be. But by the time we actually see Thomas murdered, after witnessing Part One and the sermon, we see that we knew and did not know. In the same way, the Knights and the Chorus, lacking the knowledge we have, both know and do not know what they are doing and suffering. And of course after the murder, the Knights' speeches show us yet one more aspect of the event that we knew and did not know.

It should be noted at this point that bearing witness, watching the events of the play, is from the first associated both with knowing and not knowing and with fear. In performance we are apt to be unaware of the powerful theatricality of the opening chorus. The theatrical problems of the Women of Canterbury are generally approached by way of voice production and enunciation, and we are grateful—and lucky—if the actresses recruited for the occasion manage to speak clearly and on the beat. Choral acting, as opposed to choral reciting, is usually beyond them. But Eliot understands, as no one

175

except Lorca since the Greeks has understood, that cho-
ral writing is writing for the body, and the bodily excite-
ment of the first Chorus derives from the way it joins the
feeling of knowing and not knowing to the emotion of
fear. The Chorus prefigures the action to come and com-
bines it with a bewildered self-consciousness. We move,
they say. We wait. Why do we move and wait as we do?
Is it fear, is it the allure of safety, is it even the allure of
fear? What kind of fear, what kind of safety? This is ex-
actly the question the play will put about martyrdom, put
to Thomas and to us:

Here let us stand, close by the cathedral. Here let us wait.
Are we drawn by danger? Is it the knowledge of safety,
    that draws our feet
Towards the cathedral? What danger can be
For us, the poor, the poor women of Canterbury? what
    tribulation
With which we are not already familiar? There is no
    danger
For us, and there is no safety in the cathedral. Some
    presage of an act
Which our eyes are compelled to witness, has forced
    our feet
Towards the cathedral. We are forced to bear witness.

The opportunity for the actors is remarkable. The ten-
sion between fear and freedom on which the chorus is
grounded might fairly be called the root emotion of the
theater; it is the same emotion, for instance, that a sha-
man and his audience share when he begins to imper-
sonate the spirits that are haunting him.[8] The emotion
here is intensified through group response, beautifully

---

[8] See, for example, Andreas Lommel, *The World of the Early
Hunters* (London, 1967), pp. 80-81.

registered in the language, and profoundly integrated with the action of the play. A crowd of women huddles toward the protection of what it half senses to be a fearful place. The chorus rouses the audience toward the awareness to come, of the church and martyrdom as a painful and difficult shelter.

Thomas is an easier dramatic subject for Eliot than his later heroes, because he remains active all the time he is on stage, aggressive even while he waits and watches. He is supremely connected to this world and the next, secure in his being except for the crisis at the climax of Part One. As far as it bears on Thomas, the pattern of haunting is complete when he says, "Now is my way clear." The true nature of the shadows he must strive with has been revealed to him and he is no longer isolated. We have seen, however, that in the later dramas the pattern of haunting continues to the end of the play and works itself out in the lives of characters for whom such transcendence is not possible. I would like to urge that this pattern is also present in *Murder in the Cathedral*. The sustained pattern of haunting completes the play's design after Thomas' death, and by means of a carefully prepared shift of focus imparts to the whole drama a final richness of impression too easily neglected both in the study and on the stage. As the play finds its structure in our bearing witness to Thomas' martyrdom and, through the Chorus, associates our watching and waiting with a fear that is at times close to panic, so the haunting in the play, the fear in the way of the original title, is finally brought to bear not on Thomas but on the Chorus and on us.

The sequence of events that concludes the play, beginning with the moment the Knights attack Thomas in the cathedral, testifies to Eliot's remarkable control over the resources of his stage. Thomas cries out at length, and the

murder continues throughout the entire chorus which be-
gins, "Clear the air! clean the sky!" The stage directions
make quite certain of this. The drunken Knights, then,
take upwards of three minutes—a very long time on the
stage—to hack Thomas to death, while the Chorus
chants in terror. Beyond the insistent horror of the act
itself there is a further effect of juxtaposition achieved
between the murder and the action of the Chorus. Prop-
erly acted, the choral text unavoidably suggests that in
its terror the Chorus is somehow egging the murderers
on, that the continuing blows of the Knights are accom-
plishing what the violent, physical, heavily accented cries
for purgation call for: "Clear the air! clean the sky! wash
the wind! take the stone from the stone, take the skin
from the arm, take the muscle from the bone, and wash
them. Wash the stone, wash the bone, wash the brain,
wash the soul, wash them wash them!" The Chorus brings
to a flooding climax the ambivalent current of fear that
has haunted the Women of Canterbury from the opening
scene—attraction toward Thomas and a powerful aver-
sion from him, fear for and of the martyr. The murder is
felt not only as a protracted physical horror but as an
action in which the Chorus has participated.

The speeches of the Knights that follow are of course
sinister as well as comic.[9] The two effects are connected,
as Eliot seems well aware, for our laughter involves us,
as their fear has involved the Chorus, in aggression to-
ward Thomas. We laugh with release from the constraints
of fancy-dress. In the style they adopt, the Knights voice
our own impulse to deflate the bubble of archaism,
poetry, and saintliness. We share their animus, and their
arguments turn the point against us. They have acted in

[9] Cf. Browne on Henri Fluchère's French production, p. 60.

178

our interests, as de Morville reminds us. "If there is any guilt whatever in the matter you must share it with us."

It is not the confident Third Priest with his dismissal of the Knights as weak, sad men, who has the last word, but the Women of Canterbury, who acknowledge themselves as types of the common man, weak and sad indeed. At the end they dwell upon their fear, which is no less strong for the transcendence they have witnessed. As in all Eliot's plays, the glimpse of transcendence is in itself a source of fear for those who have been left behind. They make the point the Knights have made in argument and that the choral accompaniment of the murder has powerfully enforced:

> That the sin of the world is upon our heads; that the
> blood of the martyrs and the agony of the saints
> Is upon our heads.

I would suggest that everything that happens in the play from the moment the Knights raise their swords has been designed to give these lines a weight of conviction and a dramatic force that I hope I may by now characterize with some precision—as haunting.

The treatment of the Chorus, then, establishes the pattern Eliot was to maintain in his later drama. And the pattern in turn reflects the originality and strength of his writing for the theater. What Eliot discovered was a way to make drama out of the central subject of his poetry and criticism—the calamitous loss of self and imprisonment in self that haunts our era, a dis-ease that may drive the fortunate man to glimpse transcendence, but which even those glimpses cannot cure:

> The enduring is not a substitute for the transient,
> Neither one for the other.
>
> ("A Note on War Poetry")

179

The theme pursues Eliot in all his work. In drama, his success was to make the sense of pursuit a ground for action and the theme a source of design, to transmit to his audiences the haunting pressure of "the enduring" on those who, like us, are condemned to roles as actors in a transient world.

Donald Davie

AS A BRITON commenting on
an Anglo-American poet, I am
assuming that a little insularity will not come amiss. And
in fact it can hardly be avoided, seeing that my particular
concern is with those last poems—the *Four Quartets*—
which were undertaken by a British citizen and com-
pleted in a Britain at war, and which allude continually
to England's historic past and to what was then London's
imperiled present. This is borne out by that one of the
Quartets which seems not to fit my description; Eliot,
when he herded all his American references into "The
Dry Salvages," rather plainly meant, by thus honoring his
transatlantic pieties in one delimited act of homage, to
assert his right through the rest of the sequence to speak
as an Englishman.

Eliot had undoubtedly earned the right thus to speak
for his adopted nation; his patriotism is moving, and I
have no wish to impugn it. Yet it is certainly to the point
to ask how well he knew the country and the people that
he meant to speak for. And if I read aright the mostly
ungracious comments that may be culled from English-

men of my own generation and younger, the consensus is that Eliot knew England and the English very imperfectly, after thirty years. Some of the evidence is too familiar to be worth dwelling on—such characteristically English voices as D. H. Lawrence's, Thomas Hardy's, William Blake's, Eliot showed himself more or less deaf to. But other features of Eliot's adopted Englishness may not be so apparent to a non-British audience; and in that sentence I have slipped in one of them already—"English" and "British" are not the same, and when Eliot welcomes "regionalism" in *Notes Towards the Definition of Culture*, this is not going to satisfy people who define themselves as Scottish or Welsh, let alone Irish. Among Eliot's British contemporaries we need think only of David Jones, Robert Graves, and Hugh MacDiarmid, to be reminded how there are other ways of tying historic Britain in with European Christendom besides the one that Eliot impatiently or blandly took to be the one right way— through Canterbury and Lambeth. Eliot's sense of Britain is offensively metropolitan—and not of Britain, but of England too; his England is to all intents and purposes London, or at most the home counties.

This takes us at once into the *Four Quartets*. For are not three out of those four poems named after English places, all of them outside the home counties—Burnt Norton in Gloucestershire, East Coker in Somerset, Little Gidding in Huntingdonshire? So they are. But in the first place every one of these locations is presented in the poem as a place of pilgrimage, accordingly as seen from the outside by the visitor from London (or for that matter from St. Louis, Missouri); no sense is conveyed of what it is like in the twentieth century to *live* in these places. Little Gidding for instance has existed for the last thirty years under the roar of giant airplanes from the USAF airfield at Alconbury; what are we to make of that, or what would Eliot have made of it? And, secondly, each of these three places is well outside the industrialized Midlands and North—the areas that have been for one hundred fifty years the heart, once throbbing and now ailing, of imperial and then post-imperial England. I am not sure there is any evidence that Eliot ever traveled in industrial England at all—in that England whose damaging pressures made Lawrence's voice so shrill and yet so insistent. And in fact his leaving this England out of account, his blankness before the phenomenon of an industrial proletariat, is surely what invalidates Eliot's thinking about politics. His vision of what English society should ideally be like envisages the working-class as agricultural, and the worker as peasant. Ireland in Eliot's lifetime had, as it still has, a peasantry; England had not, and has not. Charles Maurras in France, like Yeats in Ireland, was prescribing for a society that comprehended, and largely rested upon, a peasantry. It might be argued that Eliot as a political thinker made an initial miscalculation that bedevilled him to the end, when he applied Maurrasian categories to a country, England, where the peasantry was long extinct. And in that case one reason for Eliot's remarkably sustained and virulent antipathy to Hardy might be that Thomas Hardy, though he is too often lamentably applauded as a spokesman for English peasant-culture, in fact documents with impressive sobriety and conviction how peasant and lesser yeoman alike had in his lifetime disappeared, depressed and dispersed into an agricultural proletariat.

Thus you will begin to see that when I call this essay "Anglican Eliot," I intend by that a mildly acrid pun. The more Anglican, the less English—or so I want to suggest. I speak on this matter as an Anglican myself, or rather as a member of the Episcopal Church of America. The distinction is important; for whereas the Episcopal Church of America is of course in communion with the Church of England, it is—like the Church of Ireland and the Church *in* Wales and the Episcopal Church of Scotland—disestablished, as the Church of England is not. And there is some reason to doubt whether Eliot would have joined the Church of England, if it had not been the *established* church.

This may be contested. Did not Eliot write: "One of the most deadening influences upon the Church in the past, ever since the eighteenth century, was its acceptance, by the upper, upper-middle and aspiring classes, as a political necessity and as a requirement of respectability"? Indeed he did; and made a beautifully calculated polemical elaboration of this point, observing (what is even truer now than in 1931) that a profession of Christian faith is nowadays for the English *intelligentsia* a very eccentric action indeed, and that a profession of *Anglican* faith is the most eccentric and least reputable of all. But later in the same essay—"Thoughts after Lambeth," one of the most vivacious and brilliantly vehement of all his prose performances—Eliot embarked upon a series of disclaimers such as his practiced readers long ago learned to recognize as the overture to something outrageous:

"I do not propose in this essay to enter upon the difficult question of Disestablishment. I am not here concerned with the practical difficulties and anomalies which have made the problem of Church and State more acute in the last few years; I am not concerned with prognosticating their future relations, or with offering any facile solution for so complex a problem, or with discussing the future discipline within the Church itself. I wish to say nothing about Disestablishment, first because I have not made up my own mind, and second because it does not seem to me fitting at this time that one layman, with no special erudition in that subject, should publicly express his views. I am considering only the political and social changes within the last three hundred years. . . ."

And then, after a series of knowledgeable allusions to the Laudian church of the seventeenth century, and to the Erastianism of the eighteenth, and to "Lord Rothermere's sometime nominee, Lord Brentford" (whoever *he* was), Eliot duly proceeds to the outrageous:

"Whether established or disestablished, the Church of England can never be reduced to the condition of a Sect, unless by some irrational act of suicide; even in the sense in which, with all due respect, the Roman Church is in England a sect. It is easier for the Church of England to become Catholic, than for the Church of Rome in England to become English; and if the Church of England was mutilated by separation from Rome, the Church of Rome was mutilated by separation from England. If England is ever to be in any appreciable degree converted to Christianity, it can only be through the Church of England."

It is not hard to envisage the apoplexy with which Evelyn Waugh's Roman Catholic Englishman, Guy Crouchback, might have read these bland words from the Missourian convert; nor, to move from literature into life, how they might even now be received by any scion of the Huddleston family, who as untitled gentry have held Sawston manor in the Old Faith since the thirteenth century. I do not know what the passage can mean, if not that it mattered a great deal to Eliot that the Archbishops and Bishops of the Church of England sit, as "lords spiritual," in the Higher Chamber of Parliament; or that (to put it the other way around) he would have been quite

185

unperturbed by the hackneyed British gibe at the Church of England, that it is "the Conservative party at prayer."

This is not in the least to impugn the sincerity of Eliot's conversion to Christian faith; it is merely to point out that, when it came to deciding what Christian sect he should join, it was of the utmost importance to him that he choose what should seem to be not a sect at all but a national norm, its normality shown in that it was backed by the secular and institutional forces of the nation-state. What else should we expect of the author of *The Idea of a Christian Society*?

It is important to realize just what is involved, and to do so one needs a firm sense of the very peculiar place of the Church of England in twentieth-century English life. Eliot wrote: "Anyone who has been moving among intellectual circles and comes to the Church, may experience an odd and rather exhilarating feeling of isolation." The feeling was natural, and it corresponded to the reality. For just because so many of the English respect the Church of England as a matter of form, to respect it and embrace it in all seriousness is to be thought a very odd fish indeed. Eliot found himself thus regarded, and the experience was "exhilarating." In this way, even as he gloried in not being "sectarian," he was able to enjoy the sectarian's luxurious sense of being set apart, special, even a standing reproach to others. For the second time in his life Eliot at the time of his conversion opted for isolation, for embattled independence. (The first time had been when, at the time of his marriage, he had thrown aside the academic future that he had trained for.) It is entirely natural, and yet it is disastrously wrong, to regard Eliot's joining the Church of England as the smooth culmination of a policy of playing possum by which a demurely histrionic American won to a commanding position in the English Establishment. How much more frank and brave, we may reflect, the doomed intransigence of his *confrère*, Ezra Pound! And yet just as Pound, broadcasting from Rome to the advancing American armies, conceived himself to be an American patriot speaking for Jeffersonian America against the deluded America of Roosevelt, so Eliot, when he loyally wrote pieces for *Britain at War*, for *London Calling*, or for *Queen Mary's Book for India*, was speaking, against the deluded England of such as Harold Laski, for the England of Lancelot Andrewes, of John Bramhall and Nicholas Ferrar—an England just as little known or regarded by the British soldier, as the America of Martin Van Buren was by any GI in the army of General Patton. In both cases—in Yeats's too, for that matter—we have a poet offering to speak to and for his nation, but in the service of a national tradition that each nation has, without knowing it, repudiated. Eliot might have remarked, and very forcefully too, that at least in his case the repudiated tradition persisted in the letter if not in the spirit, institutionalized—as the Church of England. Mr. Graham Martin takes the point very well when he asks: "In 1942 who but Eliot would be likely to have felt drawn away from the contemporary crisis by the 'antique drum' of Charles the Martyr's confrontation with Oliver Cromwell?" But when he proceeds at once to declare, "This aspect of the poem seems unlikely to wear well," surely we may retort that it is likely to wear as well as the Church of England has.

The cultural value of such an institution as that Church—however "ossified," however "empty," however its persistence may be "merely formal"—is something that we can find acknowledged by Eliot's peers, by Yeats and Pound. And indeed their acknowledgment of it is what sticks indigestibly in the gullet of the neo-Rousseau-

187

istic generations who succeeded them, whose simplifica-
tions we have somehow to cope with at the present day.
Yet it was in his generation Eliot who hammered this
point home most insistently. And hence the particular
venom that is reserved for him in the vocabulary of our
neo-Rousseauists. For what they cannot forgive Eliot is
that he proved his principles right in practice; that he,
alone among Anglo-American poets of his time, achieved
what (in some sense, surely) all of them were aiming at.
His is the one incontestable success-story; he spoke for his
adopted nation, and that nation acknowledged his right
to do so, for after all he *did* get the O.M., and he *is* lauded
in Westminster Abbey. How indigestible that cannot fail
to be, for those who want to recruit poetry into the ranks
of the perpetual (perpetually irreconcilable) opposition!

When I say that the English nation thirty years ago
recognized Eliot's right to speak for them, of course I am
not forgetting that the overwhelming majority in the Brit-
ish Army, the Royal Navy, and the Royal Air Force
did not know even his name. Indeed I am speaking im-
pressionistically, out of memories, and on the basis of
such evidence as the flyleaf of my copy of *Selected Essays*,
which reveals that it was purchased in Colombo, Ceylon,
in 1945, and was apparently filched by me from a mess-
mate. Undoubtedly there were many, in 1942 or 1945,
who preferred the wittily and impudently erudite young
American of 1920 to the voice of the Establishment that
spoke to us in the new poems of the 1940's. Let F. W.
Bateson speak for them, wistfully honoring the scholarly
and Laforguian impertinence of Eliot's youth: "The
scholarship, it was true, was only skin-deep, whereas the
Anglo-Catholicism was devoted and sincere, but most of
us—English and American—will continue to prefer 'The
Hippopotamus' and its progeny to *The Rock* and its suc-

188

cessors." Among those who might agree are, we may suppose, the survivors of that Bloomsbury whose *mores*, sexual and other, seem to have exacerbated (though admittedly the record is far from complete) the disintegration of Vivien Eliot and of Eliot's first marriage. In any case, the fact remains—that the author of "The Hippopotamus" could not have been the voice of an embattled nation, as the author of *The Rock* and *Four Quartets* could be, and was.

Of course, to a later British generation than Mr. Bateson's or mine, these are in any case "battles long ago." In Mr. Jonathan Raban's very sprightly and entertaining *The Society of the Poem*, published last year in London, it is hard to decide what is more remarkable—that for Mr. Raban, as for Ivor Richards nearly fifty years ago, modern British poetry should start with that American whom the late Lord Russell found so singularly lacking in vitality; or that the poems of that American which are found so momentous should still be "The Love-Song of J. Alfred Prufrock" and *The Waste Land*. It seems that our younger contemporaries are determined to hang on to the piecemeal world which *The Waste Land* presents to them, as it did to us; and that just for that reason they repudiate that world as put together again in *Four Quartets*—repudiate it, yet not with contumely. (For if there is one thing more out of fashion than Anglican dogma, it is fiercely reasoned objections to it, such as Kathleen Nott directed at *Four Quartets* a generation ago.) No, simply it is too ignominious to submit to time-honored medicine for ills which we owe it to ourselves to regard as unprecedented. And in any case it must be assumed that anything the Archbishop of Canterbury might countenance cannot be right; for the Church of England, now as in 1931, belongs for the Englishman in the world of

189

public ritual and social decencies, not in the world of real private worries and desolations.

Thus Eliot was as isolated at the end of his life as halfway through it; and the tired and devious procedures of a late work like *Notes Towards the Definition of Culture* suggest that, understandably, he found the condition less "exhilarating" as time went on. He had chosen—though (as I have argued) always on his own, quite special terms—to ally himself with the British Establishment. And in Eliot's lifetime that Establishment was, as it always is in England, non-intellectual. Like that other brilliant and quixotic immigrant, Edmund Burke, when faced with a choice between the more or less international community of intellectuals and the community of the nation, Eliot opted firmly for the latter; and was eager to defend his choice, as Burke was. Unavoidably, in both cases the intellectuals raise the cry, "A sell-out!"—from their point of view, quite properly. The heat that is engendered, even now, in both parties to the quarrel about Burke is to be expected—and no doubt it is to be welcomed—in the quarrel about Eliot.

All of this would be beside the point, it would be fruitless special pleading, if *Four Quartets* were—simply as writing, as configurations of and engagements with the English language—manifestly inferior to *The Waste Land* and other earlier poems. And of course on both sides of the Atlantic it is quite commonly said that this indeed is the case. I do not know what to do about this—in the first place, to vindicate a poet's use of language at that crucial level is something that cannot be done properly in small compass; and secondly, modesty shall not prevent me from saying that I am among those who, in the more appropriate medium of closely reasoned print, have attempted that vindication more than once. If I have not persuaded Helen Vendler on those earlier occasions, I can hardly hope to do so now.

Accordingly it seems more profitable to attend to Mr. Kenner, who believes as I do that the *Quartets* (though uneven) are a substantial achievement, and to see if we can agree on what that achievement is. In *The Pound Era* Mr. Kenner offers a sort of definition when, speaking of the *Quartets*, he says: "To unite . . . a *Symboliste* heritage with an Augustan may have been Eliot's most original act" (p. 439). And so far as "the *Symboliste* heritage" goes, we must be happy to concur: sluggishly and belatedly we have got round to recognizing that the title Eliot gave to these poems, together with the allusions that they make to Mallarmé, places them as part of the French *symboliste* endeavor to make poetry "approach the condition of music." But the Augustan ingredient in the concoction is harder to isolate. And to my mind Mr. Kenner is on shaky ground when he decides that for the *Quartets* Eliot "went to the most inconspicuous of English poets, the ones who flourished a generation after Pope and were accustomed to take up a stance in a particularized landscape and meditate." To begin with, it is not clear who these poets are. Mr. Kenner goes on to cite Gray of the *Elegy*, hardly the least conspicuous of English poets (or of English poems); but it is hard to decide what other poets of Gray's generation are meant to stand with him. "East Coker" is the "quartet" which best fits Mr. Kenner's case, as when he remarks: "Of all the famous poems that have preceded it *East Coker* most resembles Gray's *Elegy*, with its churches, its tombstone, its hallowed voiceless dead, its rustic intelligences." And we can readily agree that the two poems begin with strikingly similar sentiments:

191

In my beginning is my end. In succession
Houses rise and fall, crumble, are extended,
Are removed, destroyed, restored, or in their place
Is an open field, or a factory, or a by-pass.
Old stone to new building, old timber to new fires,
Old fires to ashes, and ashes to the earth
Which is already flesh, fur and faeces,
Bone of man and beast, cornstalk and leaf.
Houses live and die: there is a time for building
And a time for living and for generation
And a time for the wind to break the loosened pane
And to shake the wainscot where the field-mouse trots
And to shake the tattered arras woven with a silent
        motto.

But if the sentiments are like Thomas Gray's, the expression is surely very far indeed from the marmoreal succinctness of Gray's elegiac quatrains. "Succinct" is almost the last word one would think of applying to this passage, or to many similar passages in the *Quartets*; and I realize very well that this heavy stamping up and down on one spot—old this to new that four times over, and a time for this and a time for that, and to shake this or to shake that—is what exasperates many readers. Yet the effect is not one of dispersal and dilution, only of gloomy insistence. I think there is nothing comparable in Gray. But in *The Book of Common Prayer*, there is: "Lay not up for yourselves treasure upon the earth; where the rust and moth doth corrupt, and where thieves break through and steal: but lay up for yourselves treasures in heaven; where neither rust nor moth doth corrupt, and where thieves do not break through and steal." And who can miss, behind "Old fires to ashes, and ashes to the earth," the order of service for the burial of the dead—"we therefore commit his body to the ground; earth to earth, ashes to ashes, dust to dust"? Or, behind "Bone of man and beast, cornstalk and leaf," the piercing sentences from the same order of service: "Man that is born of a woman hath but a short time to live, and is full of misery. He cometh up, and is cut down, like a flower; he fleeth as it were a shadow, and never continueth in one stay"? Archbishop Cranmer and his collaborators were not succinct writers, and yet no part of *The Book of Common Prayer* is either diffuse or florid. The effect is, to my ear, that when we reach the quotation in antique spelling from Sir Thomas Elyot's *Boke Named The Governour*—

> The association of man and woman
> In daunsinge, signifying matrimonie—
> A dignified and commodious sacrament.
> Two and two, necessarye coniunction,
> Holding eche other by the hand or the arm
> Whiche betokeneth concorde—

it is as if this too were from a homily spoken in a Tudor church. And why not? Sir Thomas Elyot was Cranmer's and Coverdale's contemporary, as was Mary Queen of Scots, on whose motto, "In my end is my beginning," "East Coker" both begins and ends. It looks as if the component of the poem which is not *symboliste* is rather Tudor than Hanoverian. And in being so it is the more Anglican.

Yet of course Hugh Kenner had good reason to look in the *Quartets* for the note of English Augustanism, to look for it and even, in one sense, to find it. For there is no doubt that behind Eliot's writing in these poems there lie Johnson's "London" and his "Vanity of Human Wishes"—poems which years before had provoked from Eliot the apparently trenchant but in fact characteristi-

193

cally slippery dictum, derived from Ford and Pound,
"Great poetry must be at least as well written as good
prose." The poetry of the *Quartets* swings to and fro be-
tween the sonorous opalescence of Mallarmé and at the
opposite extreme a prosaicism so homespun as to be,
from time to time, positively "prosey" or "prosing." It is
at or about this prosaic pole of the poems' language that,
as Eliot says, "the poetry does not matter." And it is this
pole of the language that can be charged by the insistent
explicitness of the Anglican homiletic and devotional tra-
dition. It was because Gray typically and expressly ig-
nored this prosaic pole of poetic diction that Johnson, in
his Life of Gray, cavilled at all Gray's poems except the
Elegy. And of course it is Johnson, not the Erastian Gray,
who represents the Hanoverian Church of England at its
noblest and most humane. For already, ten years after the
death of Pope, English Augustanism is no longer homo-
geneous but splitting into opposed camps, Johnson and
Goldsmith on the one hand, Gray and the Wartons on the
other; and Eliot as critic ranged himself firmly with John-
son and Goldsmith. Thus there *are* Augustan principles
at work in and behind the poetry of the *Quartets*, but they
are the principles of only one wing of late-Augustanism,
the wing that was, both politically and poetically, con-
servative (whereas Gray in his time was thought of—and
rightly—as a radical innovator). Because it is conserva-
tive, Johnson's Augustanism is not specifically Hanover-
ian but takes pride in holding true to a tradition of prosaic
verse which reaches back, in the *Lives of the Poets*,
through Denham and Cowley even to Donne, a tradition
which there is no difficulty about tracing back, with Ben
Jonson and Ralegh, to Tudor times.

　　This is something more than captious in-fighting between me and Hugh Kenner—to whom, as it happens, I feel myself under a greater obligation than to any other critic of the *Quartets*. For it is only if we insist on the prosaicism of much of the *Quartets* that we can recognize the high tension set up between this element and, at the other pole, the Mallarméan. On the one hand a form that is musical, non-discursive, on the other hand a content that for long stretches is painstakingly discursive, even pedestrian; on the one hand Mallarmé, by-word for poetry that is all implication and suggestion, on the other hand Cranmer, bleakly and unsparingly explicit; on the one hand nonce-words like "a grimpen" and unseizable sonorities like "The loud lament of the disconsolate chimera," on the other hand—

> There are three conditions which often look alike
> Yet differ completely, flourish in the same
>   hedgerow . . . ;

on the one hand poetry at its most private, on the other hand poetry at its most public and, for the sake of being public, prepared to dispense with most of its customary ornaments and splendors.

It is small wonder if the product of such extreme tension is a poem remarkably uneven in tone if not in quality; a poem which has to make a formal virtue out of its own disparities, by inviting us to think that it switches tone only as Beethoven does when he completes a slow movement and embarks upon a scherzo. What interests me more is to ask how a poet could ever get himself in the situation of creating such a tension and attempting to resolve it. And I conceive that this might come about if a poet, compelled by temperament as well as history to school himself in the ironic reticences of Henry James on

195

the one hand and Jules Laforgue on the other, should find himself wanting to speak to and for a nation which conceives of itself as cornered into a situation that is wholly unironical because not in the least ambiguous. For such a poet (who may be wholly imaginary) I should feel affection as well as esteem.